© Cherry Publishing, 2024
for the English translation

ISBN: 978-1-80116-738-3

1

Joy

After almost three years at college, my time in Lincoln is slowly coming to an end. This summer I will be graduating with a degree in psychology and moving to California. Even before I started studying in the north of the USA, I knew that I wanted to settle down in California one day. It's still a few months away and I want to spend as much time as possible with my friends - Phoenix, Millie and Sienna. We've really bonded over the last year and a half. Then there are their boyfriends Jake, Denver, Darren and Tyler. The fact that six of the eight of us are in relationships and that Denver and Phoenix are siblings doesn't always make things easy.

I met Phoenix at a party in my second year and through her I met her brother Denver, Jake and a little later Darren. When Sienna came to Lincoln a year and a half ago and accidentally got the empty room in Denver's apartment, she joined our group and Millie joined soon after. Tyler was the last to join. He transferred from Ohio State University to Lincoln College and completed our octet. Since Denver and Sienna, Darren and Millie, and Jake and Phoenix are a couple, Tyler and I are always on the outside looking in. I don't really mind. I can even understand why they would rather sit with their partner than me on a night out or at dinner.

The problem is my past. Unlike the others, I didn't meet Tyler in college, but much, much earlier.

Our regular diner is a fifteen-minute walk from campus on a quiet street. Denver's pickup and Millie's Porsche are parked outside. I push open the front door and a small bell signals to the staff that I have entered. My friends are sitting in an alcove at our regular booth. The guys are very well known at the college, so fans - yes, they already have fans - come up to our table all the time, asking for an autograph or a photo. I sigh as I see my friends. Tyler is already sitting at the table and, as usual when we all get together, there is only one empty chair and it's next to him.

Sometimes I feel like the girls are pushing our relationship a little bit because I have to sit next to him or ride with him all the time. They don't realize that I don't want to. I'm not like Millie, who gave Darren another chance even after he ignored her a hundred times, or Phoenix, who had the patience of a saint with Jake until he finally realized she was the one for him.

Tyler and I go back six years. We went to high school together and spent a summer together. Then, overnight, he moved to Ohio with his parents without telling me. It wasn't like he had three whole months to tell me.

Since Tyler's been in Lincoln, I've tried to avoid him. Which is total bullshit because Denver, Jake and Darren of all people have become his best friends. None of these guys will be able to relate to my resentment and, instead, will make me out to be "vindictive". What can I expect from three hormonal football players for whom sex is their second favorite sport? It is truly a miracle that all three of them are in committed relationships. Especially Darren. He's the one I least expected to be faithful. But he and Millie are perfect for each other. He loves her to death.

When I ran into Tyler on campus a year and a half ago, I was speechless. I couldn't believe he was back in my life after all these years. At first, he didn't recognize me. It was no wonder, since twenty-one-year-old me and fifteen-year-old me have very little in common. Back then I wore my natural black hair and my style was simpler. The last time I saw him, I hadn't yet dyed the tips of my hair. They're blue now, but maybe I'll change that. And while I used to be ashamed of my Asian roots because they didn't fit the outward ideal of an American woman, I now embrace them. My father's ancestors are from Shanghai and came to the U.S. as children after World War II. They settled in a small town in Kentucky. My mother's family is American. My parents met in college when my father was studying medicine and my mother was studying philosophy. Like Tyler, I don't have any brothers or sisters. This makes me enjoy being with my friends and Phoenix's family even more. I only fly to Kentucky for major holidays and my parents' and grandparents' birthdays.

I don't remember exactly when Tyler recognized me, but at some point, he stood in front of me and wanted to know if I was "Jolene Lin". His Jolene. My heart started racing and I couldn't do anything but nod. At first, he seemed reserved, but then he started talking to me and said we should meet. I turned and left. I didn't want to talk to him or listen to a word he said. Besides, he calls me Jolene, which no one in Lincoln does. I'm Joy to everyone here and I want to keep it that way. Despite me telling him not to call me Jolene, he still does. It's bad enough that my parents call me by my real name. I can do without it in college. It doesn't suit me. Too well behaved and too well-mannered. Everything I'm not anymore.

Joy is better and trendier.

Besides, Tyler lost the privilege of calling me Jolene when he disappeared the morning after we first had sex to move to Ohio with his parents. To this day, I haven't given him a chance to explain, and I won't. I don't want to hear his excuses. I don't want him to tell me that he was only seventeen and had to go with them. I don't doubt it at all. It's obvious that he couldn't stay in Kentucky by himself when he was seventeen. My only issue is that he didn't say anything in all the weeks we were together. He should have. He didn't even bother to stop the charade until I gave him my virginity. I was naive at the time. I thought I was sharing this special moment with a special boy. Tyler was that boy for me. And what did I get? An asshole. I should have waited. My first boyfriend, Anthony, would have been a much better candidate. Instead, I slept with Tyler and am forever tied to the memories of that night and that jerk.

Tyler's dad was a doctor at the Army base in Lexington while my dad was in the hospital there. We lived on the same street and had known each other for years. Of course, when his dad got transferred to Ohio, it meant that Tyler and his mom had to move with him.

Looking back, I'm not sure I wouldn't have slept with him anyway had I known. The fact is, I was very much in love with Tyler, and maybe I still am. No one has been able to interest me in anything more than sex in the last few years. Despite my relationship with Anthony, Tyler was always on my mind. I've never really been able to get away from him and it's really getting on my nerves.

"Hi," I greet my friends and kiss Millie, Sienna and Phoenix on the cheek. "Sorry I'm late. Hey, guys."

I sit down in the empty chair next to Tyler and try not to show how much this bothers me. I try to ignore Tyler and hope he doesn't force a conversation on me today. Sienna says I shouldn't make such a fuss and should be friendly toward Tyler. I want to see how she would react if she were forced to sit next to Denver if he were to dump her like that.

"What are you talking about?" I ask the group, reaching for my Coke that someone must have ordered for me.

"Our vacation in Australia," Millie says. "We're debating whether to take a commercial flight or our jet."

By 'our jet', she means her family's jet.

I smile because she throws it out there so naturally like we all have the same family background. Since we found out that our Millie Mouse is a Millie Billionaire, she's been really great. Nothing seems to be too much for her - and we all benefit from that.

"Commercial flight," Darren says, and Millie rolls her eyes. "You'll survive, and business class is really comfortable."

"I can't afford to fly all the way to Australia," I say, looking at Darren. What does he think? I don't have any sponsors. I have my scholarship and my parents' money. Flying business class to Melbourne is out of the question. "And you know it."

He groans and Millie grins.

"Then let's take the jet," she concludes, taking his hand. "Joy's for the jet and Phoe and Jake too. That makes four of us."

"Denver, Sienna, Tyler and I are against," Darren lists. "It's four to four, baby."

Darren grins at Millie. It's not the grin he used to give his bedmates when he wanted to get on with things. It's a loving grin that immediately makes her sigh.

"What would be best for Charlotte?" I ask, looking at Phoenix and Jake.

11

It's still hard to believe my best friend became a mother for the first time five months ago. She and Jake are the perfect couple. Still, it took almost two years of sleeping together, a stint abroad, and a baby for them to find each other. Mostly because Jake never had the balls to stand by Phoenix and put her before his friendship with Denver. At least Jake was honorable and didn't dump Phoenix. Well, not in the traditional way. He let her flee to Bristol, England, which wasn't much better. But when she came back heavily pregnant, he immediately took care of her and their daughter Charlotte.

"The jet," Jake sighs and looks apologetically at Darren. "Sorry, dude. But it has a bedroom and we can always put Charlotte to sleep or feed her in there."

Darren mumbles something and raises his hands disarmingly.

"Fine," he grumbles. "Then we'll take the jet."

"Perfect." Millie snuggles up to Darren. "If the baby sleeps in the bedroom in the jet, that'll be fine."

"Oh yeah?" I ask, raising my eyebrows. "Doesn't anyone want to join the Mile High Club?"

There's definitely enough willing participants in the group.

"We're already members!" Darren grins so broadly that Millie blushes.

"How many times do I have to tell you to keep that to yourself?" she hisses. Millie should know after a year with the guy that he'll never learn.

"Oh, come on, Millie," Sienna says in a good mood. "Indoor pool, private jet? Where don't you do it?"

"You forgot her penthouse with picture windows overlooking Lincoln. Have you ever done it against the windows?" I ask, embarrassing Millie even more.

"No comment," she grumbles, giving Darren a warning look. "Not from you either."

"I didn't say anything," he sighs, shaking his head.

"So yes," Denver sums up their reactions and reaches for Sienna's hand. "Anyone else want to confess?"

"So, we..." Phoenix says provocatively, grinning at Jake, "did it the other day..."

Everyone knows Denver doesn't want to hear about his sister's sex life with his best friend.

"Topic over," he interrupts. "What about the trip? What did Sadie say?"

Sadie is Phoenix's girlfriend, whom she met during her Work & Travel in England. Sadie was with Phoenix for most of her pregnancy and will be meeting little Charlotte for the first time.

"Sadie is giving us two cabins on the ranch. We have to pay for food like all the other guests, but no rent."

"Is she sure?" asks Sienna. "We can pay two hundred dollars each."

"I suggested that to her," Phoenix answers. "But she doesn't want it. We'll have to split into two groups of four in the houses. But Jake and I want to take the house with one bedroom upstairs and one bedroom downstairs because of Charlotte. When Charlotte is crying and grumpy, it will be less disruptive for you."

"You know very well that Charlotte doesn't bother us," Sienna says, rolling her eyes. "The most logical thing would be for the four of us..." she points at herself, Denver, Jake and Phoenix, "to share a house because of Charlotte and the four of you." She points to Darren, Millie, Tyler and me.

I look around and am anything but happy with this arrangement. Of course, the fact that Tyler and I aren't a couple becomes a problem again. If only Millie and Darren weren't either, then the four of us could easily share a house. So, they do their couple thing and we... I don't even want to think about how much time I'll have to spend with Tyler in such close quarters.

"We can do that," Tyler agrees and Millie and Darren nod in agreement.

Annoyed, I look at Tyler and raise my eyebrows. He can't, no, he can't be serious. He has to realize I don't want to be in the same house with him. Not today, not tomorrow and not for years to come.

"What?" he wants to know. "I think the division makes sense."

"Do you?" I hiss. "Good."

"How do you want to divide it?" he asks, annoyed. "It's probably best for Charlotte to share the house with the people closest to her."

"Yes, her parents," I counter. "As far as I know, that's Jake and Phoenix."

"But Denver is her godfather," Tyler argues.

"She's not baptized!"

"Hypothetically," Tyler says. "But sure, if you don't want to share a cabin with Millie and Darren..."

That bastard! I have no problem sharing a cabin with Millie and Darren. His stupid grin tells me he knows exactly that.

"This is not about Millie and Darren and you know it!"

"Of course, I know it," Tyler says with a shrug. "We're going to be together all the time during the three weeks anyway. The nights don't matter."

Annoyed, I cross my arms over my chest.

"That sounds even better," I hiss. "Doesn't Sadie have a hot cowboy brother?"

I know she does. His name is Kyle, and he's from a good family. Maybe I should think about having some fun down under. After all, I'm single and no one can tell me what to do.

"Don't feel under any obligation," Tyler says, giving me an

irritated look. "You can sleep at his place and we can have some peace and quiet."

He's acting like a little kid, but what do I expect from him? Maturity has never been his thing. Not now and not six years ago.

"Well, now that that's out of the way, let's get on with it," Jake sighs. "We're flying during eighteen hours from Chicago with a refueling stop in Honolulu. Right, Millie?"

"Right," she confirms. "We have to be at the airport an hour before takeoff and someone will meet us there. Then we board the jet and take off."

I only listen to her with half an ear because my eyes keep drifting to Tyler. It happens all the time and it annoys me as much as everything else about him. Why can't I just ignore him? It can't be that hard, can it?

Unfortunately, I have to admit that he looks outrageously handsome today. He wears his blond hair cut short at the sides. His broad shoulders and muscular chest are visible under the hoodie with the Lincoln Tigers logo on the right chest. Tyler is damn good-looking, there's no denying that. He looked good as a teenager, but he's even more muscular now. Suddenly he looks at me and I hold his gaze for a moment. Then I look away and back at Phoenix. She grins and I sigh. Of course, she noticed me staring at him.

"Joy?" Confused, I look at Sienna. "Are you coming with me?"

"Where to?" I ask, not having been listening.

"The party," she reminds me. "Tomorrow night for the end of the season."

"No," I say. "That's for the players and their girlfriends, you know."

As expected, everyone at the table rolls their eyes, but I don't care. I'm not a player's girlfriend, and I have no business

15

being at an event like that. So, I stay home. And I don't want them to get the idea that I should go with Tyler. Because I won't. Everyone knows we're not a couple, and they would assume I was invited out of pity because my friends are going.

"But..." Sienna begins.

"I said no," I hiss. "Leave it at that."

I can see that she wants to say something else, but she changes her mind. They need to understand that Tyler and I aren't a couple and that it affects the group dynamic.

"I have to go," Tyler says, putting ten dollars on the table. "See you tomorrow night. See you, Jolene."

"I'll go with you," Denver calls out, also putting money on the table for himself and Sienna. "See you tonight, baby."

"See you tonight," she replies with a grin after he kisses her goodbye. Baby Charlotte also gets a personal goodbye from her uncle and then he and Tyler leave the diner.

The looks on everyone else's faces speak volumes.

"What?" I bark at my remaining friends. "Tell him to stop."

"Stop what?" Darren wants to know. "Making it clear that he wants to get into your pants?"

"Asshole," I growl and Sienna, Millie, Phoenix and Jake laugh. "I thought you had him under control." I raise my eyebrows at Millie.

"I did," she giggles and snuggles up to her boyfriend. How can anyone be so disgustingly happy. All six of them. "He's just telling the truth, Jolene."

"Jolene, Jolene, Jolene, Jolene ... I beg you, please don't ..."

"Shut up, Phoe," I yell, but I can't help but grin as she belts out Dolly Parton's classic.

2

Tyler

The bass echoing through the gym's large speakers is deafening. We're celebrating the end of the season, even though we didn't make it to the final game of the college championship. It would have been nice to have made it, but we lost to Arizona in the playoffs. It was a close game and maybe we could have done better in the last quarter, but there's no point in dwelling on that. We didn't make it and that's the way it's going to stay.

"Hey," Darren greets me with a handshake which I return.

I look for Millie but don't see her.

"Are you alone?"

"Yeah," he sighs. "Millie's not feeling well. Probably food poisoning."

"Or pregnant," I joke and he rolls his eyes. "Fine, not funny."

"Not funny at all," he grumbles and I grin. "Millie and I have goals. There's no room for a baby in them."

Darren has become my best friend in the year and a half

I've been in Lincoln. After transferring from Kentucky, it was hard for me to make friends in Ohio. It was the same in high school. It didn't get any better in college, so I was happy to accept the offer from Lincoln. Here I finally found real friends in Darren, Jake and Denver. Because of that, I can relate to Millie. Our situations are not comparable, but she never made friends either because she had more of something than everyone else. For her it was money, for me it was talent.

After my first party and kiss with Denver's girlfriend, Sienna, it didn't look like I would ever settle in. It was my first night in Lincoln and I was thrilled to be invited by the boys. Denver and Sienna weren't dating at the time, but my buddy didn't take too kindly to me sticking my tongue down his girl's throat. To be honest, I can't remember what made me do it. Maybe the fact that she looked really sad and I wanted to cheer her up. Whether a kiss was the best way to do that remains to be seen. Fortunately, everything worked out and Denver understood that I didn't want anything from her.

My attention is drawn by another woman - Jolene Lin.

Or Joy, as she prefers to be called. At first, I couldn't believe it was really her. I hadn't seen her for five years. We've both changed, but Joy has changed more than a little on the outside. I never thought that the doctor's daughter, who was so cute back then, would turn into a real vamp.

Joy is smoking hot and she knows it. Her dyed blue hair suits her as well as the wicked makeup and tight clothes she usually wears. She's incredible and I would give anything to feel her seductive body under mine again.

Some of the guys on the team have had sex with her. I don't like it, but I have no reason to stop them. From what they say, she's a bomb in bed. When we made love, she was cautious and insecure, like everyone during their first time, right?

We've both gained experience over the years. But darn it,

Joy doesn't seem interested in a repeat performance. Instead, she annoys me with statements like she wants to hook up with Sadie's brother in Australia. I shouldn't care, but it gets under my skin.

Back in the day, I messed up big time by leaving right after sleeping with her, leaving her in the dark about us moving to Ohio. Joy's attitude now is payback for my actions. She makes it clear every time we meet that she's not thrilled about me and would kick me out of the group if she could. But no way I'm letting her get that right. Plus, I'm not dumb—I notice her sneaky side glances.

"Millie's not pregnant," Darren pulls me out of my thoughts. "She just had her ... you know."

"Then you must have really blue balls," I chuckle and nudge him.

"I fixed that yesterday," he answers proudly. "She'd kill me if she knew I was telling you that."

"I think you've told me worse."

"Maybe," Darren says and I follow him to the bar.

As expected, Phoenix and Sienna are there. But unlike Darren, I can mingle with the cheerleaders.

"Hey, Tyler," Phoenix greets me and I hug her. I greet Jake amicably.

"Hey," I say. "Are you okay?"

"Everything's fine and you?"

"Me too," I reply and say hello to Sienna and Denver.

We're going to Australia next week and I have no idea what to expect. The six of them are all paired up, and, of course, they will want to spend their time together. Joy isn't entirely wrong when she says it's going to be uncomfortable for us. There's no way she's going to want to explore the area with me while the others are doing their couple things. Maybe I should consider canceling the trip and go visit my parents in

Kentucky. I haven't seen them since they moved back there after my dad got out of the Army. It's been almost two months.

Then I remember that this will be the last time we all go on vacation together. Our futures will be decided in April when we have to show what we can do at the Combine in early March to get the attention of NFL scouts. For Denver, Jake, Darren and I, it seems like a sure thing that we will make it into the highest professional league in the world. We've already been watched by several scouts at practice. The more interesting question is what part of the USA we'll end up in. It's unlikely that two of us will end up on the same team. Only Darren and I might be lucky enough to find a team that needs a defensive end and a running back.

"Beer?" Denver asks, handing me a bottle.

"Thanks," I say, toasting my friends as Phoenix pulls her iPhone out of her bag.

"I have to go," she says, "Charlotte's teething and she won't let my mom soothe her."

Jake gives her a worried look and pulls her a few steps away from us. Becoming a parent at such a young age isn't always easy. I can hardly imagine being a father in the next four or five years. Denver and Darren feel the same way. Jake, on the other hand, says that Charlotte is the best thing that's ever happened to him. I take him at his word, but I'm not going to copy him.

The two seem to be arguing, but eventually Phoenix kisses him and leaves alone.

"Are you staying?" asks Denver and Jake nods.

"Phoe thinks I should enjoy the evening and Charlotte won't let me calm her down anyway."

"Okay," Denver says. "Looks like I'm the only one with a date."

Denver pulls Sienna toward him with a grin.

"Was that a hint for me to leave?" she asks, raising her eyebrows. Denver shakes his head, and they share such an indecent kiss that we look away, annoyed. My buddies always have to put on a show. Darren and Jake can't help themselves either, no matter how they react.

"I need another beer," Darren decides. "Who's coming?"

"Me," I say as Jake shakes his head.

Before he met Phoenix and moved in with her to give Charlotte a real family life, we lived together for a few months. Sometimes I miss the time with him, but, of course, I gladly gave up my room for his two ladies. Now I live in a small two-room apartment near the gym.

"Millie and I have been talking again," Darren says, looking at me. "If it's really that big of a problem for Joy, then the two of us can share a room and..."

"No," I cut him off before he can finish. "She shouldn't keep making such a fuss, and the place probably has a good couch."

"But..."

"Darren, you're not seriously going to sleep in the same room with me for almost three weeks."

"No," he admits through clenched teeth. "But you know how Millie is. She doesn't like it when someone is unhappy and tries to find solutions."

My buddy clearly sounds annoyed by his girlfriend's behavior. Never in my wildest dreams would I have thought they would end up together. Millie and Darren are so different, but they're perfect for each other.

"I'll talk to Joy again," I promise him, leaving myself a little wiggle room. "If she gives me the chance."

Judging by the look on Darren's face, she won't give me a chance. Joy is ruining everyone's vacation with her behavior. I've already thought about not going, but in the end it's not an option. We're a group and she'll just have to get over it.

Anyway, in two months she won't see me again.

"Because it works so well for you," Darren teases and I groan.

"And what do you suggest? You want to talk to her?"

"God forbid," he says. "According to you, I'm the worst thing that could have happened to Millie."

"Given how you treated her according to the girls," I say, siding with Joy a little. Darren never paid any attention to Millie or talked to her, even though a blind man could see that she was in love with him. The jerk didn't even have the decency to keep his conquests hidden from her. Then, when he needed help, he remembered that there was sweet Millie to get him out of trouble. And, well, it worked in the end. "I'll talk to Joy and make it clear that she's going to ruin the vacation for everyone if she continues to behave like this."

"And you really think she'll listen to you?" he asks and I shrug.

"In the end, she knows it's a group activity, and it's not my fault that Sienna, Millie, and Phoenix all have partners."

"She really shouldn't make such a fuss," Darren says. "But you know her. If she doesn't want something, she doesn't want it."

"I know," I sigh. "Anyway, it's her decision if she comes or not. I'm not going to talk her into it."

Darren nods and we mingle with the party guests again. It doesn't take long for the cheerleaders to realize that Darren and Jake are alone. As expected, they literally throw themselves at my buddies. It bounces off them, I can tell. Still, the girls are so persistent that it's almost embarrassing.

"Hey, Tyler," a voice sounds next to me and I turn to find Cassandra. I like her and she's not as annoying as most cheerleaders. We both know that we're just sleeping together and that's fine with us.

"Hey," I greet her, "how are you?"

"I'm good, and you?"

"Me too," I reply. "What are your plans for the semester break?"

Cassandra tells me that she's going to her parents' house in New Orleans and then to her sister's house in Florida for a few days to visit her grandmother. In return, I tell her that we're going to Australia to visit Phoenix's girlfriend Sadie. I find out that she spent a few weeks working and traveling in Australia and am almost a bit sorry that Phoenix is not here anymore. I'm sure she would have been interested as well. Cassandra is, I think, the only cheerleader who hasn't been labeled by the girls. But she's also the only one who doesn't throw herself at the players.

★★★

Cassandra wraps her legs around my hips as I pump into her harder and harder. My whole body is tense and I can't concentrate on the woman beneath me, I can only think about Joy. Like so many times during sex the last few weeks. Damn it, this can't be happening. She would never think of me.

"Fuck," I growl and push harder into Cassandra. She moans and wraps her arms around my neck. Our lips collide and I increase the rhythm of my thrusts. Cassandra moans under me; at least she seems to be enjoying it. And I want to bring her to orgasm as well. Annoyed, I slide my hand between our bodies and rub my middle finger over her clit. As expected, her body tenses and her moans get louder. I thrust into her harder and let my finger circle her clit faster.

Moaning, she tightens around me and I'm almost relieved that she came so quickly. Frustrated, I let go and pull out of her.

"What's wrong?" she asks immediately, propping herself up on her forearms so that she's no longer completely on her back. "Tyler?"

I pull off the used condom and toss it in the trash.

"You should go," I say, stepping into my boxers. "Now!"

"Go?" she asks. "Why... I mean ... what's wrong with you?"

"It has nothing to do with you," I rattle off, probably the dumbest thing she has ever heard. Even if it is the truth. It's not fair to Cassandra that I'm fucking her while thinking about Joy. "I like you and you ... you don't deserve the fact that I'm thinking about someone else."

"You ... you're thinking about ... someone else?" she whispers, sounding really hurt.

If I thought 'It has nothing to do with her' was the most pathetic thing I could say, I've gone one better.

"I'm sorry," I mutter, smiling at her helplessly.

"I should go."

Cassandra gets out of my bed and I turn away so I don't stare at her as she gets dressed. Annoyed with myself, I put my hands on the desk and hang my head. I feel like a huge asshole, but dumping her wasn't fair.

"I'm sorry," I tell her again.

"Hm," she mumbles, "let's not do it anymore."

Now I turn and look at her. Cassandra looks sad. Fuck. I didn't want this to happen. I never should have used her to get Joy out of my head. It hasn't worked for months. Unless I've had too much to drink to care.

"Do you still want me to walk you to the door?"

"No thanks." Now she's getting snippy. "I can find my own way."

"I'm sorry," I say again, hoping she believes me. It was never my intention to hurt her. I like Cassandra and have always had a good time with her.

"Bye Tyler," she mumbles, "and I hope she knows how lucky she is."

I look at her for a moment and nod. No, Joy doesn't know, or rather doesn't want to know. Cassandra nods at me one last time, leaves my bedroom and a few seconds later the apartment.

"Fuck, fuck, fuck," I yell, pulling at my hair, "I'm such an idiot."

3

Joy

I step out of the bathroom in my one-room apartment that I moved into last semester when there's a knock on the door. Relieved that I'm already dressed and just need to towel dry my hair before styling it, I open the door. I'd rather close it right away because there's Darren, casually leaning against the door frame and grinning at me. I don't have the best relationship with him, to put it nicely. I consider him a clueless idiot, and he thinks of me as a sassy bitch.

Even before Millie and Tyler joined our group, I had a hard time with him. Through Millie, I learned a lot about Darren, explaining why he is the way he is. I didn't know that his parents don't support him at all and believe that football has no future. I also didn't know that he's actually a quiet guy and can be very understanding. I only found out all this from Millie, who, of course, now claims that she knew all along. Absolute nonsense, but if it makes her happy - fine. Fine with me.

Tyler and Darren have become best friends. This also makes

27

it impossible to kick Tyler out of our group. But Denver and Jake wouldn't let me kick him out either. And since he hasn't done anything to Sienna, Millie or Phoenix, he gets to stay.

Darren visiting my place can't mean anything good. He would never come willingly. Either Tyler sent him because he doesn't have the guts to talk to me himself, or Millie suggested something that he doesn't like. I'm leaning towards the latter because I can't imagine Tyler sending Darren.

"The answer is no," I say before he can get a word out.

Darren crosses his arms, emphasizing his biceps. The guy has gained a lot of mass in the last few months to make it to the NFL. He has always been muscular, no doubt, but now he's a real machine. As a defensive end, he needs that muscle mass. The offensive players in the NFL will be a different caliber than those in college. I'm less worried about the quarterbacks; he'll easily outclass them.

The thought of Millie's delicate body next to him makes me shudder. He must flatten her during sex. Having almost two hundred pounds on her. Millie weighs about half as much as Darren. She's never complained about the sex, but she has nothing to compare it to. She's never had sex with another guy.

I may sound spiteful to Millie, but secretly I'm jealous of her. Darren is the love of her life and she never gave up hope that there was something between them, despite all the adversity they've faced. I, on the other hand, lost the guy I thought was the one after our first night together. Darren Andrews, of all people, came back repentant after doing something like that. It can't be true.

"I didn't even ask you a question," he replies casually, grinning at me. "And we've known each other long enough to know that neither of us is the asking type. I can't believe that for one second I thought about taking you to my sister's wedding."

My eyes widen and I stare at him. He thought what? It would never have worked. We would have torn each other apart during the preparations or one of us wouldn't have survived the flight to Texas.

"Where did you get the stupid idea that I should go with you?" I retort. "Good thing you asked Millie."

"Yeah," he replies, and his usually cool and arrogant facade cracks immediately. Say what you will about Darren, but he adores our Millie mouse. Whenever she's by his side, he's more reasonable, nicer, and most of all, more reserved. She's good for him, and he's good for her. Darren has boosted Millie's self-esteem, and we are all grateful. Without him, I'm sure she'd still be hiding behind her books. "She was more malleable than you," he replies. "You couldn't have kept up the mask it took to pull it off in front of my mother."

"More malleable?" I ask, raising my eyebrows. "Have you told her yet?"

"She knows," he says casually, grinning at me. "Come on, Joy. We both know she wouldn't have said a word if things had gone according to plan."

"Since when does anything go according to plan?" I wonder aloud, saying it more to myself than to Darren.

"Rarely," he replies. "And I'm really glad they don't. Otherwise, my sister would be married to that wanker and I'd be..."

"You would still be fucking anything in a skirt?" I ask sweetly and grin at him.

"Exactly!" In typical Darren fashion, he agrees with me completely. He also admits that he didn't give a shit about Millie before their arrangement. Brave of him. He could have spun a tale about being too shy to approach Millie until then, but everyone knows that's not true. "May I come in?"

He nods and points to my room. I sigh and let him in.

Darren walks past me and I close the door behind him.

"I don't have anything to drink and I don't want you to sit down," I say directly, crossing my arms in front of my chest. "What do you want? I assume it's about Tyler and the trip to Australia."

"Honestly, I don't give a shit if you come or not."

"Thanks," I grumble. "It's not like we've been friends much longer than you and Tyler."

"Is Tyler being this childish or just you?" Darren wants to know. "And it's not about Tyler, it's about Millie. It bothers her that the two of you don't get along. She even suggested that she share a room with you and I share one with Tyler."

I'm wide-eyed and could kiss Millie for making the suggestion. It would definitely minimize our problems. They wouldn't be solved, but they would be a lot easier to deal with. I'd just have to get through the days without Tyler, but that would be easy. I always do what he doesn't. Unless we're traveling with the whole group and I have to go along.

"That's very nice of Millie," I say.

Darren's face falls and he visibly gasps.

"You'll talk her out of it," he growls. "I'm not sleeping in the same room with Tyler for three weeks."

"It's not that bad..."

"Then why don't you share a room with Sienna or Phoenix?"

"They have the baby," I answer. "It's not possible."

"Sienna and Denver don't have a baby," Darren hisses, visibly trying to calm himself. "Joy, it won't work and you know it. I don't want Millie and I to have to break up because of your problems with Tyler."

I look at Darren and walk past him to sit on my bed. He turns and looks at me. Of course, I don't want him and Millie to break up. I especially don't want that for Millie. She gives us so much that we could never afford with our own money.

The guys, Phoenix, and Sienna still can't. Eventually, they'll be able to rent a jet too. I, on the other hand, don't have a boyfriend with ambitions for the NFL who will earn millions. Let alone a wealthy family. It's only fair that we make it as enjoyable as possible for Millie, and that includes letting her sleep in the same room as Darren.

"So, Joy?" Darren presses on and I look up at him. "Will you tell Millie and the others that you'll go and that you'll sleep where you're supposed to?"

I don't like how he talks to me, but I don't really have a choice. Darren is right, I'll ruin Millie's vacation if I don't give in. None of the others will agree to share a room with me. They're all couples and they want to be with their partners. I could pick up a guy by next week and take him with me, but that wouldn't solve my problem with Tyler.

"Do I have a choice?" I reply, rolling my eyes. "Hardly, if you're going to go to all this trouble for me."

"It's not about me going to all this trouble for you," he hisses. "My girlfriend wants to ruin our vacation out of consideration for you. That's messed up."

"Maybe Millie understands more about friendship than you ever will," I reply snottily and stand up. "It would be really terrible if you couldn't have sex for three weeks. Blue balls?"

Darren's eyes narrow to slits. It's clear that I've hit a sore point with him about sex. Of course, he's only thinking about that and not about how I feel when I have to share a room with Tyler. He's had it easy. He was never in love before Millie, so he's never been disappointed. For Darren, life is one big party, and Millie is his personal jackpot.

"It's not about sex, and I've gone three weeks in a row without it." He rolls his eyes. "Unfortunately, Millie is too nice to tell you how shitty you are behaving. And she's missing out on having a good time to accommodate you. That's not fair."

"Only someone who's never been hurt talks the way you do," I say, pulling the towel off my head to disappear into the bathroom. I don't want my day to be completely ruined by his showing up. I'm meeting with my study group today because I have an exam the day after tomorrow. The last one for this semester and my college career. I have to pass it in order to be allowed to write my thesis. So, I don't really care if Darren is here or not. I have no intention of changing before then. Besides, I'm sure Darren knows what happened between Tyler and me. Only the sugarcoated version, of course. The poor kid who had to move to Ohio with his parents.

I look in the mirror and see Darren standing in the door-way behind me.

"What do you really think of me?" he asks, shaking his head.

"You want an answer to that?" I reply and he laughs. Darren licks his lips and crosses his arms over his chest.

"My first girlfriend left me because all I cared about was football," he tells me. "So yeah, I know what that's like. And I was about to do the same thing with Millie, and I would have lost her, too. I don't know the details of what happened between you two, but you should talk to Tyler."

"You really think that's the same?" I raise my eyebrows and laugh. "Interesting."

"I never said it was the same," he retorts, and unfortunately, I have to agree with him. "And I don't think I'm the person you want to talk to about this either, am I? I just want to tell you that I've been hurt too, because I've made mistakes. We all have, even Millie."

I say nothing, grab my hairdryer and tell him to leave me alone. I can't talk to Darren. We keep twisting each other's words. Before I can turn on the hairdryer to drown out Darren's annoying voice, he pulls the plug out and stands next to me.

"What are you doing?" I yell at him. "Can't you see I don't want to talk to you? It's nice that Tyler's gossiping about it."

"Tyler doesn't gossip and you know it," he says. "Come on, Joy."

"Everyone knows what happened by now anyway," I sigh and look at him. "What do you want from me? What else is there to talk about?"

"Not everyone knows and Tyler doesn't gossip," he snarls. "Can't you at least try to get along with Tyler?"

"Do I have a choice?" I ask again, raising my eyebrows. "We both know I don't, Darren. You said so yourself, you don't want it to ... ruin your vacation. Somehow, I'll make it work with Tyler."

"That's all I wanted," he answers with a grin and puts the hairdryer plug into the socket again. "Thanks."

I don't say anything and nod at him. Darren acknowledges it and turns around, hopefully to leave me alone to contemplate my foolish decision.

"And Joy?"

"Yeah?" We look at each other in the mirror again.

"He likes you," Darren says with a smile. "Maybe you'll at least try to give him a chance. Even if it's just on a friendly, neutral basis, for all of us."

I open my mouth to reply, but Darren turns and seconds later my bedroom door slams shut behind him.

Sighing, I put the hairdryer down and look at myself in the mirror. My hair is damp over my shoulders and the blue is a shade darker. I push it back to look at my face, which looks even more like my fifteen-year-old self without makeup. I liked that me too, but I'm happier now. At least I thought I was until Tyler came back into my life. Who does he think he is, just showing up and messing things up so much that I don't even want to go on vacation with my friends?

I sigh.

What am I supposed to make of the fact that Tyler likes me? It doesn't mean anything to me. Not now and not six years ago. He shouldn't have run away then. He could have waited until I woke up to tell me he was moving to Ohio with his parents. That's all I wanted: not to be alone the morning after. Tyler didn't do that, and that's why I can't have a friendly, neutral relationship with him.

4

Joy

Chicago Airport, One week later

Today is the day, and we are leaving for Australia. That's why I've been so nervous the last few days. I'm still a little worried about being so close to Tyler for so long. I don't want to have any contact with him if I don't have to. I was so sure that once college was over for us, I could cut him off except for a few mandatory meetings with our group. The guys will go off to the teams that drafted them. Phoenix, Sienna, and Millie will go with them and build their lives with them.

For me, it means writing my psychology thesis and getting a job. I'll probably move from Illinois to sunny California. Los Angeles or San Diego are high on my list of cities I'd like to live in. After three years in the cold North and a childhood in the Midwest, I'm ready for the Sunshine State.

"Hey," I greet Phoenix with a hug. "Hi, Jake."

"Hi," he says, giving me a kiss on the cheek. Then he turns so I can greet Charlotte, who's sitting on a carrier in front of his chest.

"Aren't the others here yet?" I ask, looking around the air-port departure lounge. Millie told us to meet here and that an airport employee would pick us up and take us to her family's private jet.

"Denver's still parking the car and Sienna's in the bath-room."

"I see," I say. "And Tyler, Darren and Millie?"

"Not yet," Phoenix answers. "I hope everything goes well with Charlotte on the flight."

I see her worried look but don't know what to tell her. Jake, Denver and Sienna will surely have been trying to reassure her the last few days, but it's not easy for Phoenix. I remember how hard it was to drag her to a party when Charlotte was much younger. We had to force her to go and leave Charlotte. It did her good.

In that regard, Phoenix is really at a different point in her life than I am. On the other hand, I'm about to graduate and she has to start all over again in the summer. Depending on where she and Jake move to, she wants to study fashion. How she came up with that is still a mystery to me, but if it's some-thing Phoenix wants, then she should go for it.

"There they are," Jake says and points to the entrance.

Millie and Darren come towards us hand in hand. Each of them is pushing a suitcase in front of them, which is of course - how could it be otherwise - from the luxury brand Louis Vuitton. Not to mention Millie's pink Birkin bag.

Tyler is walking beside them, talking to Darren.

I look at him for a moment and have to admit that he looks good. He has his baseball cap on backwards and he's wearing a black hoodie under his winter jacket. He's also wearing jeans and white sneakers. Darren is dressed similarly, while Millie is in a wool dress, over-the-knee boots, and a red coat. She has changed so much in the last year.

"Hi," Millie greets us first. "Are you excited?"

"Of course," Phoenix says, greeting the three of them in turn. Jake does the same. Then it's my turn.

"Hi," I say to Millie. "New bag?"

"Don't ask," Darren grumbles next to me. "We had to fly to New York for this damn thing because they only hand these bags over to customers in person."

"Short trip to New York," I pretend theatrically. "I feel so sorry for you. Hey, Tyler."

"Hey," he replies. "Where are Denver and Sienna?"

"We're right here," comes Sienna's voice and I turn around. Sienna and Denver are walking towards us, hand in hand. Surprisingly, they're both wearing sweatpants and hoodies, with winter jackets over them. I've opted for leggings and a turtleneck.

"You're all dressed so casually," Tyler grumbles. "I shouldn't have listened to you."

He looks accusingly at Darren and Millie.

"I told you you could change and shower on the jet," Millie defends. "Free of charge."

"Free always sounds good," Tyler replies.

"Ms. McDonald," a voice calls and a moment later a young man appears behind Darren and Tyler. He's quite a bit shorter than both of them, and it looks a bit odd as he stands between them, looking around...

"Hello, Mr. Broderick," Millie greets him. "We're all accounted for."

"Perfect," he replies. "The jet is fueled and being stocked by the crew. You're welcome to have a snack and a drink in the lounge before we take off."

"Sure," she says with a grin and takes Darren's hand. "We'll follow you."

He nods and turns again, motioning for us to follow. We do,

walking behind him like eight ducklings following their mother.

"This is so exciting," Phoenix giggles next to me. "I've never been on a private jet before."

"Get used to it," I say. "I'm sure Jake will be able to get you one soon, and if not him, then your brother."

"Then you'll also be flying to New York to pick up a handbag," Tyler adds.

"No way," Jake chimes in. "What a waste."

"The next one to gossip about me stays home." Millie turns around to face us, trying to give us a stern look, which makes us burst into laughter.

***

I follow Darren to the jet and go inside to find my friends with their backs to me again. But I ignore them and look around the amazing aircraft. The floor is covered with a white carpet that is perfect for walking on without shoes. The interior is also very spacious, at least six feet wide. On the left side is a seating area with four leather chairs and a table in between, where Millie and Darren as well as Sienna and Denver have already made themselves comfortable. Opposite is a couch where Jake and Phoenix are sitting with Charlotte, and Phoenix is helping her boyfriend get her daughter out of the carrier. To the left of the door that separates the crew area from the large interior are two more leather chairs with a table in front of them. They must be for Tyler and me.

I puff out my cheeks to avoid looking belligerent again and sit down next to him at the window. I have to admit, the jet is really something. It's huge, even bigger than I imagined, and I can't believe there's a bedroom and bathroom in the back. With a shower, of course. I can see why Millie never wants to fly commercial again.

The stewardess enters the room and introduces herself. Then the pilot comes in, shakes Millie's hand, and introduces himself to us. I had only ever heard the pilot's voice, if that, and now one is introducing himself to me personally.

Unlike a commercial flight, everything happens at supersonic speed and within minutes we are airborne and on our way to Honolulu to refuel, change pilots and fly on to Australia. From the airport in Melbourne, it is at least an hour's drive to Sadie's family farm.

"We have something to tell you," Sienna says suddenly, and I look up from my iPhone in surprise - of course the jet has free Wi-Fi. Tyler, Millie and Darren look up as well. Phoenix and Jake seem less curious.

I frown and look at my best friend. When she notices I'm looking at her, she avoids my gaze and focuses on Charlotte.

What's going on here?

Phoenix would never avoid my gaze if she didn't know what was going on. I look at Sienna and Denver. She puts her hand on his, which is resting on the table. I can't see anything sparkling on her ring finger, but I assume she's taken it off.

"What is it?" Millie finally asks.

"Well," Denver says, squeezing Sienna's hand. He looks over at her and grins, which she returns. "I guess we weren't paying that much attention a few weeks ago."

I furrow my eyebrows, wondering what he means, and then it hits me like a tone of bricks. I clap my right hand over my mouth and dig the fingers of my left into Tyler's forearm, causing him to yelp.

"Ouch!" He looks at me, annoyed. "Is that necessary?"

Only now do I realize what I've done, and I let him go as quickly as I grabbed him. "Sorry," I mumble half-heartedly and pull back to my usual distance from him.

"I'm pregnant," Sienna announces and immediately starts to cry. "We... so Denver and I... we... we're going to... so we..."

She takes a deep breath and tries to control her emotions, but it's hard.

"We're going to be parents," Denver finishes the sentence.

"That's so great," Millie squeals, jumping to her feet. "Let me through, let me through."

Tyler and I can't help but laugh out loud as she pushes past Darren and tries to shove Denver out of the way to congratulate Sienna. She throws her arms around her neck and kisses her on the cheek. Sienna is still crying like a baby and when Darren gets up, Tyler and I get up and walk over to them.

"After you," Tyler says with a smile, gesturing for me to go first.

"Thanks," I say, glancing at Phoenix and Jake who are grinning broadly. He's put his arm around her and pulled her close. "You knew, didn't you?"

"Sorry," Phoenix says, raising her hands. "They told us last week at a family dinner."

I nod in understanding. Phoenix is Denver's sister, and, of course, the family finds out before their friends. Besides, it must have reminded my best friend of her own unexpected pregnancy. Unlike Sienna's pregnancy, Phoenix's was anything but planned. But...was it planned for Sienna and Denver?

"Congratulations," I say to Denver and hug him. "Well done."

"Thanks," he says before I hug Sienna.

"Congratulations, sweetie. Are you happy? How far along are you?"

"Thank you," she says, wiping away tears. "Seventeen weeks pregnant. I... I mean, we... we're very happy."

I smile at her and give her a kiss on the cheek before stepping back to congratulate Denver.

"When did you find out?" Millie asks immediately, taking Darren's hand. "And was it planned?"

"We've known since Christmas, almost two months," Sienna explains. "I was so sick in the morning and then I did the math and realized I didn't have my period..."

"I know how it is," Phoenix says lightheartedly.

"Was it planned?" I ask. "Charlotte's birth traumatized Darren, Tyler and Denver so much."

"Did you hear her scream?" Darren asks, looking at me. "It was inhuman."

"I was also in there with her," I remind him. "And yes, I did."

"It wasn't planned," Denver answers my question. "Not at all, we both wanted to wait, but then it happened."

"I know," Jake says, "and you were freaking out about going without sex less than four weeks before Christmas."

He laughs cheekily, which makes me grin too. I can just imagine that was Denver's biggest problem.

"Did you?" Sienna asks accusingly and Denver shakes his head.

"I'm so happy for you," Millie says. "Do you know the gender yet?"

"Yes," Sienna answers, biting her lip so as not to give anything away.

"And?" asks Darren. "Girl or boy?"

"One of the two," Denver answers and Darren rolls his eyes.

"One of the two?" interjects Tyler. "We weren't expecting that."

"We know," Sienna explains. "But we're not telling you."

As expected, we all purse our lips until Darren speaks.

"I'm taking bets," he says suddenly. "Who's in for a boy, an heir?"

"You can't be serious," Sienna cries indignantly. "You're

not going to bet on the gender of my child."

"See," Darren says with a shrug. "Phoenix and Jake don't know either?"

"No," Denver answers, and Sienna looks at him accusingly. "What?"

"You're not getting involved in this crap, are you?" she wants to know.

"Of course, I'm getting involved," he replies and gives her a kiss. "I would bet on the gender of Darren's child in a heartbeat."

"Idiot," Sienna grumbles, rolling her eyes.

"I don't think that's okay," Millie chimes in, looking at Darren. "It's not nice."

"Since when am I nice?" Darren wants to know and kisses her. "So... Jake, Phoe? Are you in?"

"Sure," Phoenix says. "Girl. Charlotte needs a cousin."

"Boy," Jake objects.

"I say boy too," Tyler adds his vote. "And you?"

He gives me a smile and I return it. I tap my chin with my index finger to look more thoughtful. Finally, I look at Sienna again to see if I can read something in her eyes. But she's still offended.

"I think it's going to be a boy, too."

"Really?" Phoenix asks. "Darren? Millie?"

"Girl," Darren says. "Denver didn't conceive a progeny."

"What does that mean?" he says. "You're a really great friend."

"Is that a hint?" Millie giggles. "I'm saying it's going to be a girl."

"I can't believe you're all going along with this stupid idea," Sienna sighs. Denver leans over and gives her a soft kiss. Sienna kisses him back and rests her head on his shoulder.

"Do you want to get married?" I ask.

"Let's not get carried away," Denver replies indignantly. "First the baby, then we'll get married."

"But please don't take too long and let me know in time so I can get a dress." I'm not serious. I'm the last one to panic over a dress.

"Me too, please," Millie agrees. "Let's see which one of us gets married first."

"Are you hinting at something?" Jake grumbles, "Or pressuring someone?"

Millie rolls her eyes and shakes her head.

"No," she says indignantly. "I don't want to."

"Really?" Jake presses until Phoenix slaps his arm.

"Leave her alone," she says. "You're embarrassing her."

"And I need money," Darren counters. "I need to earn the money for the engagement ring."

The private jet rings with friendly laughter, with Sienna laughing again. Now Millie is offended.

"You're an idiot," she mutters, crossing her arms over her chest. "I don't need it."

"Of course not," Denver almost sneers. "Whose jet and twenty thousand dollar handbag is this again?"

Millie actually raises her hand and gives him the middle finger.

5

Joy

Melbourne, Australia

The drive from the airport to the family farm took almost two hours. Phoenix had already mentioned that the farm was in the outback, but I hadn't expected them to take it so literally. Most of the landscape seemed very barren to me. There was hardly any grassland to be seen until just before the farm, but that changed abruptly when the small town, which is in the immediate vicinity of the farm, appeared in front of us. I estimate it to be much smaller than Lincoln. Maybe ten thousand people at the most.

"Finally, here!" Millie smiles and I nod. We unbuckle and open the doors. Tyler is sitting up front next to Darren. I was wary of the car with the steering wheel on the wrong side and I'm glad I didn't have to drive. Darren didn't mind and drove well.

Sadie parks next to us and gets out with Denver. Sienna, Phoenix and Jake are in the back with Charlotte.

I look up at the white wooden house with a gray slate roof

and a wraparound porch.

"This is our house," Sadie says, smiling as she approaches us. "Your houses are at the back of the property. However, my mom has taken it upon herself to prepare a little barbecue for you."

I nod and look at Darren and Tyler who are unloading our luggage from the trunk.

"Leave your luggage in the car," Sadie says. "You can drive the cars around back and unload them later."

"If someone else can drive," I mutter and immediately get a dirty look from Tyler and Darren. They must have gotten up on the wrong side of the bed again. But the fact is that nobody can drive the car to the back after the barbecue.

"And what do you think?" Sadie turns to Darren. "Is it like back home in Texas?"

I want to raise my eyebrows as he puts his hands on his hips and looks up at the house with a thoughtful expression. If I didn't know better, I'd say they were flirting with each other, but that's absurd. Sadie is being polite and Darren is genuinely interested. Millie seems to think otherwise, jealously grabbing his hand.

"It's a simple wooden house," she snaps at Sadie, causing Tyler to gasp next to me. Yes, it is unusual for Millie. Usually, she's the one telling everyone else to behave better. "Nothing that will impress Darren. Are you coming?"

He looks at his girlfriend, then at Sadie, then nods and lets her pull him toward Denver and Sienna.

"What was that?" Sadie mumbles, looking at me in confusion.

"I don't know," I reply. "Your mom made a barbecue?"

I hope Sadie will take advantage of my distraction and stop worrying about Millie.

"Yeah," she says, laughing. "My brother had to take a cow

to the slaughterhouse for the meal."

"Oh," I gasp. "That sounds expensive."

"Oh no..." Sadie waves it off. "We would have done it anyway and... there he is..."

What do you mean, there he is? I thought we met Sadie's brother at the airport. There wasn't any mention of another.

"Scott!" She spreads her arms and Tyler and I turn to follow her with our eyes. Coming towards us ... an incredibly hot guy! Short blond hair, a three-day beard, and a mischievous grin on his lips. Kyle wasn't my type with his brown hair, but this guy is really cute. Maybe I can make my plan to distract myself from Tyler with Sadie's brother come true after all.

"Hey," Scott replies, hugging his little sister. "You're here already?"

"Just got here," Sadie answers. "Kyle is still in Melbourne with Pete."

"I see," Scott says, taking off his work gloves and shoving them into the back pockets of his ripped jeans. He has black boots on his feet. The closer he gets, the more attractive I find the guy.

"Hi," he greets us. "I'm Scott. Sadie's brother."

He offers me his hand in a friendly way, which I immediately accept.

"Hi," I reply. "I'm Joy."

"Nice to meet you," he says, turning to Tyler. "Scott, hi."

"Tyler," he grumbles and I raise my eyebrows because now he's the one who's being incredibly unfriendly. What's going on with my friends? I mean my friend and Tyler. Sadie and Scott are super nice and hospitable.

"Come on," Sadie says, grabbing Scott's hand after he lets go of Tyler's. "I'll introduce you to the others."

Scott gives me another smile and then lets his sister pull him along.

"Jerk," Tyler growls next to me and I give him a questioning look. "Let's go join the others."

"Do you have a problem with Scott?" I ask, raising my eyebrows in amusement. "He's nice and good-looking, isn't he?"

Yes, I can't resist mentioning how good-looking he is in my eyes.

"If you say so," Tyler mumbles. "I guess that makes your intentions clear."

He leaves me standing there. If the situation wasn't so absurd and ridiculous, I'd actually laugh.

Scott is way too old for me. How old will he be? Thirty or thirty-five. Definitely not my age.

★★★

The barbecue that Sadie's parents have prepared for us is incredible. There are five different salads, plus baguettes and finger food. Sadie was not exaggerating when she said they slaughtered a whole cow just for the evening. It is delicious and we have a great time. Millie seems to have calmed down after her little jealous outburst when we arrived.

"Would you like some more wine?" Tyler holds the bottle out to me and I nod, reaching for my glass. He pours it for me and I smile at him. Of course, we're sitting next to each other again because our friends strategically placed us, leaving us no other choice. We're joined by Sadie, her mother Francis and her father Harry, and Kyle, Scott and their friends.

"Thanks," I say. "Do you like beer?"

"I prefer it," he replies, winking at me. "Although I don't know what to make of this Australian beer yet."

"From the look on your face, you're probably not that impressed," I chuckle, wondering in the next moment why I'm acting so stupid. I'm not the kind of girl who giggles because she's talking to a hot guy. The other women at the table do that. What he said wasn't even that funny.

"No," Tyler says, taking the last swig from his bottle. "It's certainly better than wine."

"Hmm." I sip from my glass and put it back on the table. "Remember that weird wine Mrs. Bishop used to bring to our street fair?"

I have no idea why I'm suddenly talking about the old days. It was years ago, and sometimes it's better to let the past be the past and not dwell on it. Tyler's and mine should just stay in the past. But I've started the conversation now and it would be silly to shut him down if he answers.

"The old dragon," he replies, rolling his eyes. "She used to chase us boys away because she thought we weren't worthy of it."

I laugh and take another sip of my wine. Mrs. Bishop was a very peculiar woman who seemed old to me even back then. But she always had an incredible amount of wine, and I know my mom used to buy some from her. The bottle my friend Kayla took, though, was disgusting. We took one sip and it almost made us sick again.

"She was always nice to Kayla and me," I think. "Her wine was awful."

"You didn't smash her living room window with a football because you wanted to practice punting."

I laugh out loud, causing Sienna to look over at me for a moment. Yes, things between Tyler and I are extremely weird right now. We haven't spoken, let alone laughed, in a year and a half. If I were her, I'd look just as skeptical. I smile at her and playfully point at her water, causing her to roll her eyes and look away.

"You did what?" I resume our conversation. "How did it happen?"

"Jason and I set everything up in the backyard," Tyler tells me. Jason was one of his buddies from high school. I don't think they were as close as he is with Darren now, but they were friends. "Everything went according to plan until Baron punted. The ball flew and flew and eventually, there was this very, very unpleasant sound of windows breaking and then she came running like a madwoman across her yard to the fence with the ball. Baron and Jason took off."

"Of course, they did," I conclude. "I would have done the same."

"Oh yeah?" Tyler grins and takes another beer from the middle of the table. "I thought you'd own up to what you'd done."

There is a split second of silence between us. Because Tyler's sentence can be interpreted differently than it was meant. In fact, I could interpret it differently. I stand by what I do. He doesn't, but if I say something, the last few minutes will have been for nothing.

"Jolene," he starts, and now they are really for nothing! He shouldn't call me that. "I mean Joy, I..."

"Hey." Scott sits down next to me on the other side and smiles at me. "Am I interrupting?"

"No," I answer immediately, glad to have the tension between Tyler and me broken.

"Do you like the wine?" he asks kindly.

"Oh, uh..." A little overwhelmed, I nod. "It tastes good."

"Great, I'm glad," he replies. "It's from friends of ours. They make wine."

"Oh, cool," I say. "In Kentucky, where we..." I'm about to point at Tyler to include him in the conversation when I realize he's not sitting next to me anymore. I look around the yard and find him at the barbecue with Sadie's dad and Denver. I can't help but notice that he's looking at me, too. What the hell is going on? First, he calls Scott a 'jerk' and then he disappears as soon as Scott sits down next to me and starts a nice conversation. He hasn't done anything to him and it would be really nice if Tyler could give Scott a chance.

"I was just going to say where Tyler and I came from, but he's not here anymore." I look at Scott apologetically, even though there's no reason to. "Tyler and I are from Kentucky and there aren't many vineyards there."

"I have to admit, they live two hours west of here," Scott says. "They sell our meat and we sell their wine. It's a win-win situation for everybody."

"I believe you," I reply with a smile, and he does the same.

Scott is nice and genuinely attractive, but still not Tyler. I look at him again and see that he's still watching me. I quickly turn away from him and back to Scott to continue our conversation. He tells me about the farm and life in the outback, which, unlike his sister, he has never left outside of Melbourne, where he studied agriculture and economics. He also does bull riding in his spare time, which I find very risky and dangerous, but Scott waves it off with a grin.

"And you've never fallen off and hurt yourself?" I ask. "You're kidding, right?"

"Of course, he's kidding," Sadie interjects. "He's bruised and broken his ribs several times."

"That's not an injury," Scott says, rolling his eyes. I laugh and look at Tyler. I've tried not to look at him, but he keeps magically drawing me back to him. Needless to say, it annoys me to no end. Not only here, but also at home in Lincoln, I find myself looking for him all the time. Especially at parties where there are lots of other women interested in him. Deep down, I know I don't like it. But I can't admit it.

But there's no sign of Tyler.

"Where is Tyler?" I ask Sadie.

"He just left," she says, "right after Sienna and Denver left."

Only now do I realize that Millie and Darren and Phoenix and Jake aren't here either. Did they just leave me here or what?

"Where are the others?" I ask. "Millie, Darren, Jake and Phoenix."

"Jake and Phoenix left before Denver, Sienna and Tyler and Millie and Darren..." Sadie shrugs in annoyance. "I really have no idea what a cool guy like Darren sees in such a condescending and spoiled bitch."

"Do you mean, Millie?" I ask, utterly bewildered, raising my eyebrows.

"Of course, I mean Millie," Sadie replies irritably. "You can't please her; nothing is good enough or worthy of her."

"You can't mean Millie," I reply, getting up. "I should go too."

"Why?" Scott asks, looking at me. "I thought we were having a good conversation."

We were, but somehow, I don't like the way things are going here. It may sound strange, but Millie isn't acting like Millie, Tyler is in a bad mood, and the other four just seem to be doing their thing.

"I know," I reply, folding my hands in front of me. "I'm sorry. I should probably go check on my friends..." Yeah, what should I do? Check on them? The siblings raise their eyebrows. I'm not their babysitter or need them to dictate how I spend my time here.

"Do what you want," Sadie sighs. "But tell Millie I'm not interested in her airs and graces. If she's not happy here, we'll be happy to give her the address of the nearest luxury hotel in Melbourne."

"Sadie," Scott hisses. "She's our guest and..."

"She's a spoiled brat who has no idea what it means to live

in the outback," she hisses at her brother and rushes off after grabbing two bowls of salad.

Must be something in the air out here.

I look cautiously at Scott. He has his hands on his hips, licking his lips when he suddenly bursts out laughing.

"Okay, wow," Scott says, continuing to clear the table. I help him. "These next three weeks are going to be very interesting."

6

Joy

A few days later

Millie, Darren, Tyler and I are heading to the coast for some surfing. Sienna isn't feeling well, according to Denver she was sick last night and is in bed. He wanted to stay with her, which I can understand. It's difficult for Phoenix and Jake to go surfing with Charlotte. So, they stayed at the farm.

After Darren parks the car, we get out to rent boards and wetsuits at a surf shop that Sadie recommended. I've never surfed before and have no idea what to do. In my opinion, it would have been wiser to hire a surf instructor to show us the ropes and warn us about the dangers of the ocean. There are supposed to be sharks off the coast of Melbourne, but Tyler and Darren already know how to surf and can handle everything. I think it's all just hot air, but okay! They know better! And I don't need to emphasize how much this annoys me, especially with Darren.

Millie has been in a bad mood since we left. Actually, she has been since we landed in Australia and Darren exchanged the first three words with Sadie. I'm starting to wonder if it's just because she doesn't like Sadie or if there's something more going on between her and Darren. But to be honest, I can't imagine that. To me, they have the perfect relationship. They're young, they have a lot of money, they're living their dream and unlike Phoenix and Jake and soon Sienna and Denver, they're completely carefree. It's a mystery to me what serious problems they could possibly have.

I shoulder my bag and follow Darren and Tyler to the surf shop. The guys lead the way and greet the clerk warmly. He recommends boards and hands out wetsuits in our sizes. We secure our bags in lockers. Armed with wetsuits, we head to the changing rooms.

"I feel like Catwoman," I exclaim as I step out of the changing room in my skin-tight black outfit. Millie does the same. Hers is red and fits her body like a second skin. It has long arms and legs.

"Sexy!" Darren walks over to Millie and pulls her against him. She snuggles up to him and plants a kiss on his lips. The two of them tune out Tyler and me, completely caught up in their world.

Tyler's wetsuit, like mine, is black. His legs and arms are completely covered. I look at it for a moment and realize that it doesn't leave much to the imagination. The wetsuit is skin-tight and clearly emphasizes Tyler's physical assets in a rather explicit way. Broad, muscular shoulders and arms. His pecs, belly and legs also stand out. There seems to be something particularly large between his legs that I don't want to look at too closely. He catches me staring and my thoughts race wildly. It's been years since I've seen Tyler naked.

"Catwoman?" Tyler picks up on my words and grins at me. "You look pretty hot, though."

I hope I don't blush or that he notices how much I like his

compliment. My heart starts to beat faster as I feel his eyes on me. Tyler makes no secret of the fact that he is looking at me closely. He even lets his gaze linger on my breasts for a moment before looking back into my eyes. He licks his lips with a grin.

"I'm hot too," I reply. "If I stand here any longer, I'm going to melt."

"Obviously, we don't want that," he answers. "Shall we go? I think they need some more time and space."

Tyler nods at Darren and Millie who are still kissing.

"Sure." I grab my board and follow Tyler down the beach to the water. "I've never been on a surfboard before."

"I did it once in Florida," he tells me. "But that was years ago. We'll just give it a try."

"On vacation?" I ask. Despite telling myself otherwise, I'm still very interested in what he's been up to all those years we didn't see each other.

"Spring break." He winks at me. "My first semester in Ohio."

"I see," I reply. He doesn't have to say more, because everyone knows the reputation spring break has among students in the USA. Sex and drinking. Mostly sex.

I quickly banish any thoughts of that. It's hard for me to imagine Tyler with another girl. There's always something about it that I don't like. You could call it jealousy, but I don't want to admit that. After all, I don't want anything from Tyler.

Nevertheless, our relationship has gotten more relaxed over the last few days. We talk a lot and even have fun together. I never thought it would happen, but things don't seem so tense in Australia and I'm not constantly reminded of what happened between us. Tyler and I avoid anything that has to do with the past, but that's okay.

"Why didn't you wait for us?" Millie catches up with us and

looks at us teasingly. "Or did you want to be alone?"

Her eyes flash conspiratorially and I narrow mine. She and Darren were the ones making out, blocking out everything around them. So, it couldn't have been me. Besides, she knows I don't like being alone with Tyler. Strange things always happen to my body.

"From what I saw, you were shoving your tongues down each other's throats," I whisper. "Did you find his uvula?"

"You're stupid," Millie mumbles, blushing.

"You're not blushing, are you?" I tease her, making sure Darren is out of sight and, more importantly, out of earshot before I continue. "What's going on with you two?"

Millie's head whips around and, like me, she seems to be checking to see if her boyfriend and Tyler can hear us. But they're already a few feet ahead of us with their boards.

"Darren's texting with other girls."

"What?" I yell, causing Darren and Tyler to turn around. I quickly wave them off and they immediately forget I said anything and concentrate on their boards.

"Is it okay if we go into the ocean now?" Tyler asks and I nod. Millie does the same. Works for me, we can talk.

"So..." I plant my board into the sand next to me and look at Millie. "What do you mean he's texting other women?"

"He ... he's texting a Cheryl ... she ... she works for the football team."

"As what?"

"Media consultant or something," Millie mumbles. "She advises the guys on interviews and checks their Instagram accounts."

"Okay, and Darren texts her... privately?" Oh God, I'm so bad at these conversations. Sienna and Phoenix are so much better. They're much more personable. "I mean, do they text each other when not working?"

"I think so."

"You think?" I ask. "Did you ask him?"

"Not exactly," Millie mumbles, biting her lip. "He had his iPhone on the kitchen table and when I walked by, it beeped. I picked it up to give it to him and there were messages from her on the screen."

"Millie, man...," I sigh, rubbing my forehead. "Get to the point. What kind of messages?"

"She asked how his exams went and if any more scouts had contacted him."

I listen to her patiently, wondering what to say. If she works for the guys, it's okay for her to ask. Maybe she needs to know in order to give them the best possible advice. It could be that they're friends, like Darren and I... though no, more like Denver and I or Jake and I.

"She needs to know that kind of thing, right?" I reply. "Then she's in the best position to advise him."

"Yeah, maybe, but she's not the only one."

Oh God, I'm really going to kill Darren if this is all true. I look at him and Tyler and see them balancing on their boards. They're not very successful though and keep falling into the water. It's just as I predicted, but now I have problems other than the two of them on the surfboards.

"Who else is he texting with?" I ask. "Do you really have any indication that he's ... well ... ?"

I barely dare say it, my stomach churning at the thought of Darren being so stupid as to cheat on Millie. Someone better than her will never happen to that idiot.

"A Beth," she blurts out. "I know her, she works for the college paper. We met a few times in the cafeteria. She asked about him there, too. What if the two of them ... what if there's more? She seemed very interested."

"And him?" I ask. "Did he seem interested, too? Did you

check his iPhone again?"

"No." Millie opens her eyes wide and shakes her head vigorously. "I would never do that. I have no idea if he's interested."

"I'm sorry," I step back and take a deep breath. "Then how do you know?"

"I asked him when I saw her name. He leaves his cell phone everywhere - so do I."

"And what did he say?"

"That she wanted to do an interview with him and that they would talk about it," she answers. "He then immediately changed the subject."

"What if that's exactly what happened?" I ask. "Then there really wasn't anything more to say from Darren's side. And what about Cheryl?"

"He said she works for his team and that he gets along with her," Millie answers, looking at him and Tyler. "Purely platonic, he stressed that again. Do you think he was just saying that to make me feel better?"

She looks at me with wide eyes. She's unsure, and I can understand that. Darren is incredibly handsome, popular with the girls at the college, and we all know he was always a ladies' man before Millie. I understand that even after a year of dating it still makes her feel insecure. But I don't think he's cheating on her.

"Darren is not cheating on you, he would never do that," I say clearly. "Get that out of your head."

"And why not?" she replies snappishly. "He doesn't try very hard to hide how great he thinks Sadie is. He's just like that ... maybe he's bored of me now and ..."

"Millie!" My voice almost cracks when I hear what she's saying and how bad she feels. She can't be serious. Darren will never be my best friend, but he loves her more than anything.

He's not cheating on her. "Darren came to see me before we left," I explain, taking a deep breath.

"What?" she asks, looking at him again. "Why ... why would he do that?"

"He asked me to relax about Tyler and told me that he almost lost you because he was so freaked out when he found out about your family."

"Yeah, so what?" Millie insists, tense. "One has nothing to do with the other."

"Darren loves you," I say. "Even though I was the last person to think it was possible. I believe him, he didn't want to lose you then, and he doesn't want to lose you now. He's not the type to pretend to love you ... what would he gain from that?"

"In case you've forgotten: My family can destroy his career plans forever in a matter of minutes," she retorts bitchily.

"You're so full of shit, Millie," I say. "He loves you. Anyone can see that. And yes, I'm sure he has other offers, but he wouldn't cheat on you. I don't even like Darren that much. In fact, in the current situation, I'd rather things between you ... ended. You know why."

A smile actually creeps across Millie's lips, but it disappears moments later.

"Maybe he finds our relationship boring?" she continues. "We've been together for a year."

"Stop talking nonsense," I hiss. "Darren loves you. But you can't expect him to cut off all contact with other women. Both Beth and Cheryl only seem to know him professionally. Even if one of them wants more from him. He has a girlfriend and he never tires of making that clear and demonstrating it to you. The way he looks at you, I don't believe that you're exchanging fewer affectionate gestures, spending less time together, and he's withdrawing from you. Or is he?"

"No," she admits. "And Sadie? What about her?"

"Oh, Millie..." I groan. "Talk to him. Tell him what's on your mind and how you feel. There's nothing wrong with Sadie. He likes her and he's interested in her lifestyle."

"He'll think I'm being ridiculous," she mutters and I raise my eyebrows. "You do too, don't you?"

"No," I say, pulling her into a hug. Smiling, I kiss her cheek. "I don't think you're being ridiculous, and I understand that you're worried. Who wouldn't be? But I don't think Darren is really giving you any reason to be suspicious. He gets along with Sadie, that's all."

"I hope you're right," she mumbles and reaches for her board as well. "I love him and I don't want to lose him."

"You won't," I assure her. "Now stop making a face and start enjoying your vacation."

"Okay," she says, "thank you, Joy."

"You're welcome."

I follow Millie to the water, board in hand. Tyler grins and comes up to me. He shakes his head, sending drops of water flying, running down his face and catching in his long eyelashes. My God, he is incredibly hot.

"Would you like to try?" he asks and I look at Millie again.

Darren has also come out of the water and pulls his girlfriend close to him. She smiles and kisses him. Hopefully, it will work out between them.

"Yeah," I say to Tyler, smiling at him.

"You better put your board over there. We'll take mine."

"All right," I reply and set it down in the sand. Then I follow Tyler into the water and let him help me onto the board.

★★★

Laughing, Tyler and I wade out of the water. He tosses his

board beside us as I plop down in the sand. He reaches behind his back with his left hand and opens his wetsuit. He casually lets the wet fabric slide down his torso so that he stands half-naked in front of me. He looks even hotter without the black fabric. Tyler has a perfect six-pack and the drops of water that fall from his hair onto his body and slowly make their way down, almost make me moan. He's really, really hot - fuck!

When he catches my eye and raises his eyebrows, I quickly look away. I feel like slapping my forehead with the flat of my hand. If he utters a single word, I'll sink into the ground in embarrassment. But Tyler says nothing and sits down next to me. The sand sticks to our legs and feet, forming small clumps. We are silent for a moment before he speaks.

"What are your plans after graduation?"

Surprised by the question, I look at him. Tyler smiles at me and seems genuinely interested.

"I want to go to California after graduation, preferably Los Angeles or San Diego, and work as a psychologist."

"Sounds good," he says. "Do you have any particular group of people you want to work with?"

"No," I say. "I thought about joining the Army once."

"You?" Tyler looks amused. "You used to get so annoyed whenever the Army practiced maneuvers."

I look at him and roll my eyes. Because of our proximity to the base, fighter jets used to fly over our neighborhood and I found it really annoying. Every now and then we'd even see a tank. However, I think that working as a psychologist in the army is very interesting, albeit intense. The fates and traumatic experiences of soldiers are nothing to sneeze at. Anyway, I would have good connections through my father to get a job there.

"That was annoying," I reply with a grin. "I would only be able to join the Army in Kentucky because of my dad's connections there."

"And you don't want to go back to Kentucky?" Tyler asks and I shake my head.

"No," I answer. "I love my parents, but no."

"My parents would love it if I got drafted by a club in Ohio. All they have is me."

I nod and agree. "I know that and..."

"We're leaving!" Surprised, we look up. Darren is standing in front of us with his and Millie's boards in his hands. His face is grim. "Are you coming?"

"Why?" I ask, looking past him to Millie. She's standing behind him, her arms crossed over her chest. It looks like they've had another big fight. I wouldn't be surprised if she bursts into tears.

"She's why," Darren growls. "Or stay here. Do what you want."

"Leave her alone, man," Tyler snaps at his best friend and stands up. "She didn't do anything to you."

Darren mumbles something we don't understand and keeps walking. Tyler shakes his head in annoyance and offers me his hands. "Come on," he says. "I'll help you."

"Thanks."

Smiling, I accept them and let him pull me to my feet. They and my bottom are full of sand, as is his. We both fail in our attempt to rub it off, but we have a lot of fun trying.

"Do you know what's going on here?" asks Tyler after we've started moving. He kindly carries my surfboard as well. Darren marches ahead stubbornly, and Millie follows a few steps behind.

"No," I lie. "Ask Darren."

"I'd rather not," he grumbles. "They need to work it out between themselves."

"True," I reply. "It's their business."

Silently, we walk behind Millie and Darren to the surf shop. Once there, Darren hands over the boards and silently takes ours from Tyler. Millie has already disappeared into one of the dressing rooms. Sighing, I turn to follow her when Tyler stops me.

"Joy, wait." Surprised, I stop and look at him. "It would be nice if we could continue our conversation... I ... I mean... I'm curious about your plans."

My heart beats so fast I can't get a word out. I didn't expect him to be so open with me. "Okay," I agree. "We can do that. I'll quickly change. See you in a minute."

Then I turn on my heel and disappear into the changing rooms.

7

Tyler

The constant bickering between Darren and Millie is starting to get on my nerves. I have no idea what's going on with them, but it's affecting the mood. I thought this vacation would finally make everything better. Joy is talking to me normally again. At the beach, I even felt like we might have some kind of connection. It's all the more frustrating now with the bad vibes between our friends. At least we're taking a stance albeit unwillingly. Joy doesn't tell me what's going on with Darren and Millie, even though she knows. At least she knows Millie's point of view.

"Good morning," I greet Darren, smiling at him.

"Morning," my best friend grumbles, looking up from his iPad. "Coffee's over there."

I look at the coffeemaker and nod.

"Thanks," I reply, grabbing a cup from the cupboard before sitting down next to him. I sip my coffee and watch him for a moment. Darren looks tired, like he didn't sleep half the night.

He's staring at his iPad, reading a U.S. newspaper. I hope the fight with Millie wasn't worse than I thought. Sighing, I pluck up the courage and bring it up.

"Do you want to talk about it?" I ask. "What's going on with you two?"

Darren looks at me and shakes his head. I wasn't expecting anything different. He's not the type to talk about his relationship problems with others. You always have to pull it out of him. Although I'm no better when it comes to Joy. I don't want to talk about what's going on between us either. It's complicated and discussing it with our friends doesn't make it any better. "I'm sorry," I say. "Forget that I asked."

Darren looks at me and suddenly grins.

"How are things with Joy?" he asks surprisingly. "You had a good talk yesterday."

"We did." A broad grin creeps across my face, not unnoticed by my best friend. "Until you came."

He sighs.

"I'm sorry," Darren says, and I can tell he means it. "But we... we fought. Again."

"Again?" I ask. "Yes. It seems to be... difficult here, but..."

"Not just here," he says, hanging his head. "Millie thinks I'm cheating on her."

My face drops, and I would have spit out my coffee if I had any in my mouth. Millie thinks Darren is cheating on her? That has got to be the most ridiculous thing I've ever heard. Yes, he always runs his mouth more than is good for his relationship. With Joy or Phoenix, his crude remarks wouldn't be a problem, but Millie is different. And Darren still flirts with other girls because he can. But he would never cheat on her. Now that she's in his life, he tunes out everything around him and only has eyes for Millie - and she only has eyes for him! I can't believe it.

"You're kidding, right?"

"Do I look like I'm kidding?" he growls at me, rubbing the bridge of his nose. "Sorry."

"It's all right," I soothe him. "What makes her think that?"

"I trust her and leave my phone lying around both at home and here," he tells me. "Millie even knows my code, it's not an issue for me. Unfortunately, lately she's had my phone in her hands every time I've received messages from other women."

"Seriously?" I ask. "Why are you texting ..."

"Tyler," he immediately cuts me off. "The messages were from Cheryl. We get along, there's nothing going on."

"Hm," I reply, nodding. Cheryl is our social media consultant and we all get along very well with her. As far as I know, she's single but has never shown any interest in a player. Especially not Darren. "That's ridiculous, and who else are you texting?"

"Beth from the newspaper," he groans. "She wants to interview me. I think she likes me. Her messages have been obvious, but I haven't paid any attention. I love Millie."

"And now the common ground with Sadie," I finish and Darren nods. "I guess that doesn't reassure her."

"Not at all," he mutters. "I also have no idea where she is. Is Joy still asleep?"

"Yes," I say. It feels strange to be able to answer that question so easily. It wouldn't have been possible before our trip to Australia and our sharing a room.

"Okay," Darren says, closing the iPad. "Maybe she's with Phoenix. I don't care."

"You do care," I scold him. "You're..."

"Okay, I care," he cuts me off. Then he finishes his coffee and puts the cup in the sink. "But how is this going to work in a few months if she's already going crazy while we're still living together? She doesn't trust me, Tyler. Maybe she never did, I don't know. But I'm not going to be accused of cheating. I don't, I never would. If there is any doubt in my mind about us, I'll end the relationship. I've seen what cheating did to my sister.

"Maybe talk to her again," I suggest. "Do something together, just the two of you, and..."

"I'll ask her."

The front door slams shut, and we turn our heads as Millie appears in the kitchen. She's wearing shorts, a top, and has AirPods in her ears. Only when she notices us does she take them out and place them on the kitchen island next to Darren. "Good morning," she greets us with a smile. "Did you sleep well?"

Jesus, this situation is so awkward. You can almost feel the tension between them. And I'm in the middle of it. Great, just great. Joy never shows up when you need her.

Darren looks at his girlfriend and almost imperceptibly shakes his head. Millie grabs a coffee and joins us. Bailing with some excuse is not an option. I don't want Millie to know that Darren told me what's going on between them.

"Morning," I hear Joy's voice and exhale a breath I didn't realize I was holding. I let my eyes roam over her body. She looks damn hot again in the short denim shorts and the low-cut top, showcasing her breasts perfectly. She has her hair pulled back in a ponytail, the turquoise tips falling over her shoulders. "All good?"

"Good, and you?" Millie asks, turning to her. "What do you want to do today?"

I look at Darren, who shakes his head again and goes back to his iPad. Millie doesn't seem to want to do anything with him. I look at Joy who looks back at me. I have no plans for today and would probably join the majority, as I have been doing the last few days. Maybe we'll see the Joneses with their partners. Sienna, Denver, Jake and Phoenix are making themselves scarce and are totally focused on doing their family thing. If things weren't so bad with Darren and Millie, it would just be Joy and I.

"Scott wanted to show us some bull riding," Joy suggests. "We could go with him to practice and have a barbecue afterwards. Maybe the others will join us."

"Scott," I scoff. "Cool."

I can't resist making a snide remark about him. The way he flirted with Joy the first night when he could clearly see me sitting next to her and talking to her didn't exactly win me over. The guy is a total creep. I don't want Joy falling for him.

"What's your problem with him?" Joy asks. "It's nice that he wants to take us."

"Really nice!" I saw the guy undressing her with his eyes the first night. His interest in her certainly has nothing to do with a friendly practice visit. He doesn't want all of us there either. He likes her and he wants to fuck her. Just the thought of her letting him fuck her makes me sick. I know I have absolutely no reason to make a scene - quite the opposite. In the past few days, we've only just managed to get back to a point where we have a friendly-neutral relationship. My jealousy is completely misplaced. I'm attracted to Joy, more than ever. And the fact that she goes to bed with me every night and yet remains unattainable is driving me crazy. The last thing I need is this Scott guy hanging around.

"Sounds good," Millie says. "We'll come with you."

She puts her arms around Darren's neck and grins at him. He meets her gaze and plants a kiss on her lips. "You should take a shower," he murmurs to her, but not so low that Joy and I hear every word. "And so should I, as it happens."

Millie giggles, grabs her AirPods and iPhone, Darren grabs his iPad, and they disappear.

"What did I do to deserve this?" Joy mutters, pouting. I laugh and look at her. "At least things seem to be going better between them."

"Yes," I say, although unfortunately reality is very different. But I won't betray Darren with Joy. "Let's go check on the others. With a baby and a pregnancy, they surely won't be fooling around."

Joy laughs and nods. "Good idea," she says. "Nobody really wants to hear that."

★★★

We ended up in a bar in the small town, inevitably close to the farm. Even Jake and Phoenix are there. Sadie's parents are watching Charlotte, on the condition that they will call if anything happens and Sadie doesn't drink alcohol so she can drive Jake and Phoenix home. I have a beer in front of me and watch Joy dancing with Kyle, Sadie's other brother. Their hips sway seductively from side to side. If I didn't hate dancing so much, I'd walk up to her and pull her away from the O'Malley brother. What does she see in these outback guys? Sure, they're not bad-looking, but what can they offer her but cow dung and wasteland.

"Hey." Phoenix appears in my view. "Are you sulking?"

"Should I be?" I ask, taking a sip of my beer. "Where's Jake?"

She points to the bar where her boyfriend is standing with Denver, talking to Scott. Everyone seems to be in love with the guy except me. Not Darren, but I don't know where he is. Either he and Millie are having sex again or they're fighting. They have these two extremes with each other. When Joy and I came back this afternoon, he was coming down the stairs. In boxer shorts, of course, and grinning stupidly at us.

72

"How's it going with Joy?"

"Great," I mutter and look in her direction again. At least she's finally put some distance between herself and Kyle. Thankfully, the song encourages it. It's much faster and has more beats. The next slow love song has them back together again. I tell myself I don't care, but it doesn't work. She should just let him fuck her. When I look around the bar, there are some cute Australian girls here. "You used to be more discreet," I accuse Phoenix.

"Very funny," she says and tilts her head. "Were you discreet with me and Jake?"

"How can you compare that?" I ask, raising my eyebrows. "That idiot got you pregnant."

She immediately swings and punches me in the chest.

"Ow," I yelp immediately. "That hurt."

"Good," Phoenix hisses. "Don't ever say that again. Charlotte is the best thing that has ever happened to us."

"I know," I reply with a smile. "Still, you could have packaged it better. It was such a ... a mix of ... of ..."

"Joy and Darren?" she suggests and I laugh out loud.

"Yes," I say and Phoenix joins in. "Exactly that mix."

"They probably can't stand each other for the same reason," she giggles, winking at me. "They're too alike. I was serious. Is it going better?"

"What do you mean better?" I laugh out loud. "Millie and Darren mostly keep to themselves and enjoy their vacation. You keep to yourselves. We inevitably get stuck together, but yes, it's much better."

"That..." Phoenix tries to explain, but I immediately cut her off.

"It's okay," I say. "You're a family. You don't have to apologize, but the arrangement is bringing Joy and I closer together."

"And that's good or bad?"

"I think it's good," I say and order another beer. Phoenix orders water. "Yesterday we had a good conversation, and she's not ignoring me or constantly snapping at me anymore. That's a success."

Jake comes up behind Phoenix and hugs her. He pulls her to his chest and crosses his arms over her shoulders. Phoenix puts her hands on his forearms and laughs softly as he kisses her cheek and whispers something in her ear. I watch my friends a little, no, very enviously. Then I turn away with my beer and get up from my seat. I guess that's the end of the conversation with Phoenix. I'm strolling through the bar when a blonde catches my eye. She's wearing jeans, a black top and her hair is styled unusually for this place. Grinning, I slip my free hand into my jeans pocket and walk towards her. If Joy can have fun with Kyle, I can have a little fun too.

"Hi," I say to her.

She looks up at me with a smile. "Hi," she says, "you're not from around here, are you?"

"No," I reply. "I'm from the States."

"Oh." She giggles. "You're one of Sadie's friends."

"Exactly," I confirm. "I'm Tyler."

"Sophie," she introduces herself and offers me her hand. I take it.

In the next moment, I experience a vivid flashback. I'm transported back to the backyard of the fraternity house a year and a half ago. Only back then, my chosen blonde conquest was named Sienna and not Sophie. I look at Sophie, trying to read her eyes to see if she's secretly attracted to another guy. I can't afford another flirtatious mishap.

"And you're from here, I take it?" I ask and she nods.

"My parents own a grocery store here in town," she explains. "We do business with the O'Malleys, as does just about everyone else in the area."

"I see." I nod at her. "Kyle or Scott?"

Sophie raises her eyebrows and gives me a puzzled look. She can't be serious. She must know what I'm getting at, right? One of them must have captured her attention. She's gorgeous and definitely single. It would make sense for her to hook up with one of them.

"Neither of them," she mumbles, blushing. I can see it even in the dim light of the bar. Her lie is exposed, but who am I to question it? It's enough that everyone else falls at her feet. "Honestly."

She looks around frantically. Her eyes sweep past me to Kyle and Joy. They're still dancing together.

"That's Joy," I tell her. "A friend."

"Okay," Sophie says. "Listen Tyler, either we leave together or I leave alone, but I'm leaving now."

More than surprised, I look at her and weigh my options. If I stay here, I'll have to watch Joy and Kyle dance and flirt some more; plus I'll have to put up with Phoenix and Jake's first couple's vacation and Darren's mood. I have no idea what's going on with Sienna, Denver and Millie, but it's definitely not going to get any better. So, I could go somewhere else with this beautiful Australian and make good use of the beds Down Under. I grin at Sophie, draining my beer and setting it down on the table next to her.

"After you," I offer her. "I'm not from here."

She grins at me, puts her glass next to mine and pulls me out of the bar with the hand behind her back.

8

Joy

Minutes must have passed as I watched Tyler and the blonde leave the bar together. Long after they left, I stand motionless on the stage. It's not a new and shocking sight for me. Tyler has sex, I have sex, and we watch each other. At least in a metaphorical sense. Until now, I've always looked at it from a certain distance, telling myself that it's okay because we have nothing in common but our past. But today things are different. Since we've been in Australia, we've been spending a lot more time together. Even if it's by necessity and even though we don't talk about what happened between us six years ago, we've become closer. You could even say that we are on our way to becoming friends. Which makes it all the more upsetting that he left the bar with another woman.

I hadn't taken my eyes off Tyler all night. Even though I was having a good time with Kyle and really like him, my eyes kept going back to the bar where Tyler was sitting. I even considered going over and having a drink with him so we could continue our conversation from the beach. I remember him saying that he wanted to know more about my plans. My damned heart beat faster. Just like it has for years when he's around. Then as now, I'm reacting to Tyler and I don't like it. I especially don't like it when he approaches random women and disappears with them. What does he think? That he's God's gift to women?

Fuck - yes! That's exactly what he is.

All the women who hit on him, whether here or in Lincoln, do it for a reason. I would do it myself if I didn't know him so well. Sometimes I don't know if he has any idea how hot he is and what effect his charm has on women. Tyler is polite, kind and decent. He's also insanely sexy and handsome. It's a deadly mix. Now this blonde is falling for his charms.

Annoyed, I leave the dance floor and go to the bar.

"A tequila," I order.

Someone sits down next to me and I slowly turn my head. My best friend looks at me with a grin.

"Two tequilas," Phoenix orders.

"You're drinking?"

"Jake's on baby duty," she explains, "and you look like you need a shot with your best friend."

"Did I hear best friend?" Sienna appears between us. "Hey," she waves the waiter over. "Give me a water in a shot glass, please, and we'll all pretend it's not water."

He raises his eyebrows and looks at Sienna like she's crazy. Granted, she might be. "I'm pregnant," she adds.

"Oh, sorry," he says. "Coming right up."

Phoenix and I laugh quietly. Moments later the shots are in front of us. Sienna grabs the one in the middle and smells it. "Water," she says, and we take the other glasses.

"Without me?" Millie squeezes between Phoenix and Sienna. "Hey," she calls to the waiter. "Whatever this is... one for me, too."

"Uh," he mumbles, clearly confused. "Water or tequila?"

"What?"

"Do you want water or tequila?" he asks. "They have both."

"Tequila," Millie says, still confused, which makes us laugh again. The waiter sets the glass down in front of her, and she reaches for it. "Cheers then!"

"Cheers!" Phoenix raises her glass and we do the same. "To the men we love and the jerks we get."

"Phoe!" Sienna shouts. "What are you talking about?"

"I'm not talking about me," she says, giggling. "I'm past that."

"At least one of us is," Millie grumbles, and we down the tequila and Sienna her water. While the three of us grimace in disgust, she cheerfully places her glass on the bar.

"Darren's not a jerk," Millie retorts. "It's normal if... if things aren't perfect sometimes."

I know for a fact that Phoenix and Sienna see it differently, but neither of them says anything. Neither do I. Instead, I order another shot of tequila.

"I can't have another one," Phoenix says, raising her hands apologetically. "Sorry!"

"I'll have another one," Millie decides, and I point at the waiter with two fingers. He pours the tequila and pushes the new glasses over to Millie and me. "All right," Millie sighs. "To the men we love and the jerks ... whatever."

We laugh and wash the shot down again.

"What's wrong with you, Millie?" Sienna wants to know sympathetically.

"She thinks Darren's cheating on her," I interject, because otherwise Millie will ramble on instead of getting to the point. "Which even I think is nonsense."

"Do you really think that?" Sienna wants to know. "I hate

to agree with her, but it's nonsense."

"I don't know," Millie says, telling Sienna and Phoenix the whole story. Like me, they both think it's nonsense - a figment of her imagination. They say they don't believe it and that she should talk to Darren.

That's the end of the subject and we fall into a discussion about what we want to do over the next few days.

★★★

I climb the last few steps up the porch to our house and am surprised to see Tyler sitting there. Shouldn't he be with that blonde Australian girl he hooked up with? Maybe he just quickly nailed her behind the bar and that was it. To let off steam or something. Who knows. I don't want to dwell on it. It's none of my business. Even though I'm burning with curiosity about what happened.

"Hey," he says, looking at me.

"Hey," I answer quietly, heading for the front door.

"I wouldn't go in there."

"Why?" I pause before reaching for the doorknob.

"Let's just say." Tyler grins and stands up. "They're having another makeup session."

"Oh." I look at him and can't help but grin. "How long do you think it's going to take?"

Tyler shrugs.

Why am I so nervous all of a sudden? It's a feeling that takes hold of me from the inside. And I don't like it. This isn't who I am. It's like being in love. Sienna, Millie and Phoenix are in love, but I'm not. They've been nervous around their crushes, but I haven't. Besides, Tyler is not my crush. What kind of crappy term is that anyway? He's my crush? Birds flock together. Many, many birds make a flock. You can't compare the two. On the other hand, butterflies also live in flocks, and they say that when you're in love you have butterflies in your stomach. The animal world confuses me.

"Jolene!" I jump, looking up at Tyler. Suddenly he's standing right in front of me. I blink and take a step back, feeling like he's way too close. I can feel the warmth emanating from his body and smell the alcohol he drank tonight. Did he drink it with her?

"Yes?" I whisper. "I was thinking."

"What were you thinking about?" he asks. "Darren and Millie?"

My head falls against the door behind me and I have to look up to meet his eyes. A smile plays around Tyler's lips and he tilts his head slightly. If he leaned down just a little bit more, he could kiss me. His lips would be on mine again. My body tingles and an unexpected nervousness spreads through me. It's been six years and I wonder if his kisses feel the same.

"Maybe we still have something to learn," he snaps me out of my thoughts.

The idea that I could learn anything from Darren and Millie is completely absurd. At least on this subject. Maybe I can with other, much more emotional topics. If I were more like Millie, I'm sure I'd fall in love and have a relationship. I have offers. But I'm not like that and I don't want to be disappointed like I was back then. It's weird to have these thoughts in the presence of the person responsible for them.

"Did you know that Darren was going to take me to Texas?" I ask and he nods.

"He asked us," Tyler says. "Who he could take. It was between you and Millie."

"Why?" I ask, grinning at him. Tyler answers.

"Well," he begins, licking his lips. "He had sex with all the other girls on campus. Except you, Millie, Sienna and

Phoenix."

"That's actually true," I reply, shaking. "My God ... how can anyone let Darren Andrews fuck them ..." A shiver runs down my spine and I squeeze my eyes shut to get the thought of sex with Darren out of my head. I mean, yes, he's super good-looking, but other than that, I can't imagine sex with him being at all fulfilling. Unlike Millie. And that's why it's a good thing he chose her.

"I think at least two hundred female students and the en-tire cheerleading squad can give you an answer to that," Tyler speculates.

"And Millie."

"And Millie," Tyler agrees. "And she's the only one who doesn't want to."

"True," I say, smiling at him. "But two hundred? Do you really think there were that many?"

Tyler moves away from me and takes a few steps back. He puts his hands on his hips and shakes his head. "Are we really talking about two hundred students letting Darren... mount them?"

"Yes." I walk toward him. "It's crazy! He's a real jerk once he's... done. He doesn't even say thank you."

"You say thank you after sex?" Tyler asks, raising his eye-brows. "Tell me more."

I look at him questioningly. When exactly did we get to the point where we're talking about my sex life and preferences? Actually, we were just joking about Darren and Millie.

"I'm not saying..." I shake my head and follow him to the seat on the porch. "Why are we talking about this?"

"Why not?" he wants to know and I sit down across from him on the small table and look at him. Tyler meets my gaze and leans back. Usually, I'm the last person to be shy or un-comfortable talking about sex. But right now, with him, I don't want to talk about it. It could lead to us talking about the past. I tilt my head slightly to look at him. "Better than speculating about Darren."

"I bet you know more than you want to."

"I do," he admits. "But I'm not telling you."

"Bro code?" I raise my eyebrows. "It's been broken before in this group."

"Denver and Jake?" Tyler asks and I nod. "That was too much, although Denver generally seems to go off the deep end when it comes to his 'women'."

"Oh, right," I muse. "You stuck your tongue down Sienna's throat."

That fact still leaves a bad taste in my mouth. Because I still don't know if she's his type. Long blonde hair, fair skin. The exact opposite of me. Just like the woman tonight.

"Don't remind me." Tyler rolls his eyes.

"Why? Isn't she your type?"

I immediately regret asking. I don't care if she's his type or not.

Tyler raises his eyebrows and leans towards me. As he straightens up, his knees touch mine. I jolt, trying to ignore the butterflies in my stomach.

"No," he says. "She's not. I don't even know why I kissed her."

"And today?" I bite my tongue abruptly. Why am I even asking? I must be crazy. It's none of my business what happened with her and I should be careful not to open this discussion.

"Sophie?" He raises his eyebrows. "She looked good, yes."

"Obviously," I mutter. "That's why you immediately left with her."

And I just keep talking - great!

Tyler furrows his eyebrows and looks at me for a moment

before suddenly laughing.

"Are you serious?" he wants to know. "You've been throwing yourself at Kyle all night and now you're accusing me of having fun."

"What?" I ask, looking up at him as he stands up and walks a few feet away. "I wasn't throwing myself at Kyle. Just because everyone in this house seems to have a problem with the siblings who put us up for free doesn't mean I do."

"And what about Scott?" he snarls. "You let him hit on you the very first night. What about the threat you made when you said you wanted Sadie's hot brother to fuck you?"

I jump up, gasping for air. Tyler's accusations hit me out of left field and I can't believe he's saying this. I didn't actually mean it and - okay, fine, I did mean it. But only to get those indecent thoughts about him out of my head that have been haunting me ever since he reappeared in my life.

"It was a joke," I cry. "I never wanted to go to bed with Scott ... and ... and even less with Kyle."

"Well, then," Tyler scoffs. "It's all settled."

"Absolutely," I hiss. "I'm going to bed and hope Millie and Darren are done."

"What's your fucking problem, Joy?" he asks. "You fuck guys as they come and I... I fuck too. What do you want from me? Why are you the way... you are?! Why does everything... really everything has to end in an argument?"

"Because you're an asshole," I yell at him. I can't believe he's making me cry. "Because you ... you're to blame for everything. I always wanted to save myself for the right guy. I ... I wanted to do it right. Then ... then you came and ... and sweet-talked me all summer and ... and then you fucked off to Ohio. Now ask me again what my problem is, Tyler!"

9

Joy

Lexington, Kentucky, six years ago

I paced nervously up and down my room. Through my window I can see our driveway, where Dad's black Mercedes is parked. There's no sign of Tyler. As soon as I think about him, I get these familiar butterflies in my stomach. Butterflies fly around and my heart warms. I should feel stupid standing here thinking about him. But I can't help it. Tyler and I have known each other for years. Our fathers work together. My dad at the hospital and his dad at the nearby army base. Tyler and I grew up together, but the fact that he's two years older than me has always stood between us until this summer. Which is not surprising. He's one of the coolest guys at Lexington High School and could have any girl he wants. He doesn't have to be interested in the fifteen-year-old daughter of his parents' friends, or rather his father's co-worker. At just under five feet tall, with chubby hips and Asian features inherited from my father's side of the family, I don't scream blonde cheerleader bombshell. I'm rather inconspicuous and don't want to stand out. Tyler, on the other hand, stands out whether he wants to or not. His broad shoulders, which are quite impressive for a seventeen-year-old, and his chiseled upper body, that he proudly shows off after training. He definitely falls into the dreamboat category, and I'm not the only one who thinks so.

This dreamboat has been spending almost every day with me since the beginning of the summer. Unfortunately, it ends on Monday and school starts again. A new school year, Tyler's last. After that, he'll be off to college and away from Lexington.

Everyone is sure he will get an athletic scholarship and continue to play football in college. Tyler wants to go to the NFL and his parents support him. Like me, he is an only child.

The roar of an engine makes me jump and run to the window. Tyler's pickup is parked behind my dad's Mercedes and he gets out. My heart rate immediately accelerates and I bite my lip. He looks insanely handsome in a baseball cap with the high school football team logo emblazoned on the front, a white t-shirt that hugs his toned chest perfectly, and beige shorts.

"Jolene," I hear my mother call. "Tyler's here!"

"Coming," I shout, whirling around to face my mirror. I cast a final glance, smooth out my short blue summer dress with spaghetti straps, slip into my sandals, and sling my bag over my shoulders. Tyler and I plan to go boating at my parents' dock. It's silly, but perhaps a romantic moment will unfold on the lake, and he'll kiss me. My heart starts racing again at the thought. I've overheard other girls talking about Tyler's prowess as a lover. Being a virgin and utterly inexperienced probably won't work in my favor. What can I offer a guy like Tyler? A little kiss should definitely be on the cards, though.

"Jolene." My mother's voice echoes through the house. "Tyler's waiting."

"It's okay, Mrs. Lin," I hear him say, and I can't help but grin.

"Coming," I call, rushing out of my room. I run down the stairs to him. He's standing at the bottom of the stairs with his hands in his shorts pockets, grinning at me. The butterflies in my stomach go crazy.

"Hey," he greets me.

"Hi."

I glance at my mom, who's still standing next to Tyler. Then I walk down the last step of the stairs and Tyler hugs me.

"Hey," he whispers again. "You look great."

"Thanks," I whisper, heat spreading through my cheeks. "You... you...too."

He smiles. "Thank you."

"Have fun, kids," my mother interrupts our greeting, and the heat in my cheeks continues to rise. I'd completely forgotten about her when Tyler hugged me to his strong body. "Bring her back to me in one piece, Tyler."

"Mom," I squeal, and I'm sure my cheeks have turned another shade deeper.

"Of course, Mrs. Lin," Tyler replies nonchalantly. "Jolene's in good hands with me."

"I know," she giggles, "I'm just kidding."

"Mom," I mumble, still embarrassed. "We're... we're going now. I'll... I'll call if... if it gets late."

If it gets late? Oh God, I really have to get out of here. There's no way it's going to be late, because there's no reason it would.

"Of course, honey." Mom grins contentedly.

"Let's go." I gruffly grab Tyler's hand and pull him out of the house behind me, laughing.

***

The downpour that descends on Tyler and me is relentless. Within seconds, we are soaking wet and barely make it into my parents' boathouse. Laughing, he slams the door behind us and throws my bag on the floor. "Oh, boy!" Tyler runs his hand through his hair *and I watch in fascination. "Even my hat couldn't protect me."*

"Right." *I look down at myself. The dress sticks to my breasts, stomach and thighs like a second skin. My hair is completely ruined and it doesn't take long for a puddle to form beneath me.* "This is not how I imagined it."

I try to pull the wet fabric away from my thighs so it doesn't accentuate them, but it's no use. I'm soaked through and feel terrible. Tyler, however, looks as good as ever. The soaked T-shirt has become transparent. It sticks to his upper body and leaves nothing to the imagination as to what he looks like underneath. Strong pecs and erect nipples, draw me in, along with his unmistakable six-pack.

"How did you imagine it?" *he murmurs to me.*

Tyler's words snap me out of my thoughts and I look up. He's standing right in front of me. So close that his wet chest almost touches my breasts. The water rolls off his hair and falls onto his cheeks, which are covered in a shadow of stubble. I can only repeat how beautiful he is. I felt like an ugly duckling next to him. I hope he doesn't tell anyone about this embarrassing outing and how foolish I am.

"Jolene?" *he whispers and I raise my eyes to meet his. I love the blue of his irises. They engulf me like a damn ocean, completely capturing me, and I have no chance of escaping.* "How did you imagine it?"

"Not so... so wet." *I giggle and Tyler laughs too.* "The downpour was a surprise."

"Hm," *he says and I could swear he takes another step closer.* "And without the downpour and the fact that we're soaking wet?"

Damn it! What does he want to hear now? I am not confident enough to give him an answer. Of course, I could tell him to kiss me, but that wouldn't be right. Tyler doesn't want to kiss me. To him, we're just friends. No matter how long I've been in love with him. And that must be two years. That's when he kissed me on the cheek at my parents' barbecue and told me I was the best. I was thirteen and he was fifteen. From then on, our lives went in completely different directions. I continued to be the unpopular girl with ugly Asian roots who tried to hide them, and he was the football star. Now, two years and many experiences later, we stand here looking into each other's eyes after a downpour. It could hardly be more clichéd. Unfortunately, this is not a romantic movie, but reality, and in this reality, there will be no Jolene and Tyler.

"I don't know," I answer his question and look at him again. "I can't tell you."

"Okay," he mumbles, pulling me closer. His hands burn a memory into the wet skin of my hips and his warm breath brushes my face as he leans in. Tyler lowers his head further so that his lips touch the tip of my nose. I giggle and inevitably dig my fingers into the wet fabric of his shirt. "Joy," he whispers, and I'm surprised he even knows my nickname. He always calls me "Jolene," and he's the only one who doesn't make me cringe. When your parents name you after a Dolly Parton song, you've really lost.

"Since when do you call me Joy?" I want to know.

"Should I call you Jolene?"

"Are we really talking about my name?" I blurt out and Tyler laughs.

"No," he says. "What I want has nothing to do with talking."

My heart threatens to explode in my chest and it's beating so fast I'm afraid Tyler might hear it. His words go through me like an electric shock. I clench my fingers in his shirt, making him laugh softly. Then he bridges the last few inches and gently places his mouth on mine. It's a shy, almost chaste touch and yet it's everything to me in this moment. Damn, this feels even better than in all my fantasies. I've had a few, but none of them had us soaking wet in my parents' boathouse.

Tyler moans softly as he deepens the kiss, pulling my body closer to him. I kiss him back, letting his tongue in and savoring the feel of his lips on mine. His hands claw harder into my hips and as he pulls *me against him, I feel his hard cock against my stomach. Fuck! I didn't expect this. I never thought it was possible that I could make him so hot. Our tongues play with each other, teasing each other, trying to get the upper hand. It soon turns out that Tyler has the upper hand. He dominates the kiss and I let him. He pushes me further back until I feel the sofa bed against my calves. We use the boathouse as a guest house when Dad's brother and his wife from Shanghai are here for a few weeks. Tyler's hands wander. He runs them down my sides, over my thighs, and grabs the waistband of my dress. My pulse quickens and I break the kiss. I hadn't expected any of this to happen between us, and I need a moment to catch my breath.*

"Joy..." Tyler pulls his mouth away from mine and looks at me with a grin. "We won't do anything you don't want."

"No," I exclaim and regret it immediately as he grimaces and tries to pull away from me. "I mean, I... I've never. You... you know."

Oh dear, this is more embarrassing than I imagined. I don't think he'll laugh at me and leave now, but it still feels weird telling him I'm still a virgin. Tyler doesn't say anything about my confession, but pulls me close and kisses me. I wrap my arms around his neck and snuggle against him. Gradually, I become more immersed in the experience and enjoy his touches on my body. "I'm going to take your dress off, okay?"

His voice is excited and gives me goose bumps. Unable to say anything, I nod and raise my arms so he can pull it over my head. The wet fabric falls to the floor and Tyler looks at me in my beige underwear. I'm glad I put on a matching set this morning. With the lace and the decorative bow between the bra cups and on the waistband of the panties, it's actually quite sexy. At least Tyler seems to like it, because the corners of his mouth turn up immediately. "You look hot," he whispers against my lips and claims them again.

We kiss again and he slowly pushes me back onto the sofa bed behind us. I fall onto it and slide back enough to lie down comfortably. A bed, preferably Tyler's, would have been nicer, of course, but

I'm not going to complain. There's no way we could do what we're doing here in either of our houses. My mom would have one ear glued to the door.

I look up at Tyler and he smiles at me. In one smooth motion, he pulls the wet t-shirt over his head and tosses it next to my dress. I stare at his muscular torso and a small "Wow" escapes my mouth. He looks amazing. Tyler grins as if he's heard my reaction clearly. Then he's on top of me.

His warm body presses against mine and I spread my legs, just as I had imagined so many times before, to let him slide between them. He uses his forearms to support himself next to my head so as not to crush me.

"Are you okay?" His voice is muffled, but still loud enough for me to hear.

"Yes," I answer immediately. "I am."

Tyler lowers his mouth to mine again and kisses me softly. His hands run down my sides and he slides his left one under my back, unhooking my bra in one smooth motion. I push it off my shoulders and toss it with the rest of our clothes. Just as I'm about to cover my breasts with my hands, not sure if I want him to see me like this, he pushes them away. "Don't," Tyler whispers. "I want to see you."

I nod slowly and lower my hands. He spreads kisses over my breasts, laps at my nipples with his tongue and sucks on them. I let out a moan and push myself against him.

Tyler pulls away and unzips his shorts. He steps out of them and when I see the bulge in his boxers, I can't help but swallow. I knew he was well hung, but I always hoped I wouldn't be one of those girls who experience pain the first time. Now I see it a little differently.

Tyler comes back to me and kisses me. I wrap my arms around his neck and kiss him back. I moan at the same time as he rubs his cock against my center.

"Are you sure?" he wants to know, searching my eyes. I meet his eyes and nod slowly. There's no turning back and I want to experi-

ence my first time with him. He's the one for me, I know it. Maybe Tyler loves me too. Maybe today is the beginning of something really special in our lives.

"Yes," I confirm and place my hand on his cheek. "I'm sure."

"Okay," he says and pulls away from me. Tyler gets off the bed and bends over to pick up his pants. He takes out his wallet and opens it. I watch as he pulls out a condom. I had completely forgotten about birth control and I feel terribly stupid. I don't take the pill. There's been no reason to, and, of course, we should use protection.

Tyler throws his wallet on the floor and the condom next to me on the couch. My heart starts beating faster and the old nervousness returns. I had gotten so used to his kisses and caresses that I had almost forgotten how nervous I was. He smiles at me and it makes me feel like what we're doing is right.

Tyler pulls off his boxers and his cock stands straight up. Thick and long, it sticks out in front of his lower abdomen and I bite my lip to keep from screaming. It'll never fit inside me.

"Jolene..." His voice is soft as he addresses me and climbs onto the couch with me. Tyler spreads my legs so he can squat between them. "Relax."

"You make it sound so easy," I whimper as his tip strokes my pussy. It's still covered by my panties.

"It's okay," he whispers, leaning in towards me. His lips gently brush against mine and I moan as his tip touches my clit.

"Tyler."

My pelvis jerks up and he moans too as he repeats the action a few times. Then he stops and looks at me again. Tyler grabs the waistband of my panties and pulls them off my legs. They land with the rest of our clothes and I bite my lip as he looks at me shamelessly.

"You're so sexy," he murmurs, kissing my lips. I kiss him back and instantly relax. I've gotten used to his kisses, they don't phase me so much anymore. Neither does the touch of his hands on my hips. But when he reaches for the condom, I stiffen again.

92

"*I'm being careful.*" *Tyler is struggling to keep his composure, I can tell. No matter how solemnly he promises to be careful, in the end, it will hurt. Tyler puts the condom on and leans over me. He plants a kiss on my lips and moves his right hand between our bodies. As he begins to stroke me with his index and middle fingers, I moan. My pelvis automatically pushes against him.* "*Fuck,*" *he gasps as he slides his middle finger inside me. I've never been touched there before; I've never really dared to do it myself. Now it feels strange to have his finger inside me. Tyler moves it back and forth until it makes a smacking sound. Moisture wets my stomach and I bite my lip. It feels good.* "*You're so tight.*"

Tyler removes his finger and positions his cock. Its head touches my entrance and I can tell from the first few inches as he pushes it into me that this isn't going to be a walk in the park. "*Tyler,*" *I gasp, digging my fingers into his shoulders.* "*It hurts.*"

It hurts like hell, more than that. With every inch he pushes into me, I'm less and less able to hold back my tears. I don't want to cry, especially not in front of him. I don't want him to see that I'm not enjoying this at all.

"*Hey...*" *Tyler puts his free hand on my cheek and brushes away my tears.* "*I'll be really gentle but tell me if you want me to stop.*"

I can't breathe anymore. The pain is unbearable and I pound on his shoulders to make him back out a bit. I tell him to stop for a minute.

He gasps. "*I'm so sorry... I ... I had to do it.*"

"*Tyler,*" *I sob.* "*It burns.*"

He nods sympathetically and kisses me gently. He stays in place for a few minutes. Then he starts to move inside me. The pain eases and eventually I feel that rush everyone talks about when they say sex is the best thing in the world.

10

Tyler

"You were gone," Joy hisses. "After what happened between us, you just left me there like ... like some slut you just had your way with."

The pain and turmoil in her eyes and voice drive a stake through me. I knew I'd made a mistake by not waking her up back then. Waking her up was out of the question. I didn't want to have to justify what we had done and then move to Ohio anyway. It was a clear line I drew and even though I knew I was being an asshole and she didn't deserve it, I had to do it. It was such a dumb move on my part that I can't even put it into words now. I liked Joy even then, more than that, I was in love with her, and that summer intensified those feelings. One thing led to another at her parents' boathouse and we slept together. I had to have her and be her first. I don't regret that night, but I know what I took from her: Giving her virginity to her first boyfriend, who would stay with her afterward. The way it should be.

"I'm sorry." I can't think of anything else to say to her.

"You're sorry?" The mockery in her voice is unmistakable. "Sorry for what? That you just used me, took my virginity that I really ... really wanted to save myself for the right guy, or that you fooled me so damn thoroughly just to get laid that I still can't believe it after all these years?"

She walks past me to the porch railing and puts her hands on it. Joy stares out into the dark night and I take a deep breath. I bury my hands in my jeans pockets and follow her. "Stay away from me."

I stand at a safe distance beside her. I give her enough space so that she doesn't feel pressured by me.

"Can I explain myself?" I ask. "I know that no excuse or explanation can justify my behavior that night, let alone what happened the next morning. But please, at least let me explain the circumstances."

"The circumstances." Joy laughs and looks at me. "I'm curious."

I've known her long enough to know that her curiosity is stronger than her anger.

"You're way too curious not to want to hear it, aren't you?"

"Oh really?" she sneers, giving me a death stare.

"Yeah." I grin. "I know you, Jolene."

"Joy," she corrects me. "My name is Joy."

"I'm pretty sure your ID still says Jolene Lin, not Joy Lin."

"You want to talk about my name again, Tyler?" Her eyes flash and I remember how we discussed her nickname before the night took on a life of its own.

"You didn't mind me calling you Jolene before."

"There is no more before," she replies, looking off into the distance. "We've changed."

I can't argue with her, we have. The once shy, introverted girl has become a confident young woman. Jolene has definitely become Joy. I don't mind, I like her as much now as I did then. "We have. A lot of time has passed."

"What do you want to say, Tyler?" She looks at me again. "I know I've changed. Inside and out. Get to the point."

"Why have you changed so much?" I ask instead of finally explaining myself. "The hair, the makeup, your clothes. It's such a contrast to before."

I haven't changed as much as she has. Still the same style, the same hair. Only my body is much more muscular and toned.

"I didn't like my former self," she admits. "I hated that everyone could see my Asian roots. I wanted to be like a typical American cheerleader. Preferably blonde, with fair skin and full lips. That was my idea of what a high school queen should look like."

"Who looked like that?" I laugh. "No one."

"Sienna and Phoenix."

"Okay, fine," I back track. "But I don't understand why that is always a benchmark for girls. Most cheerleaders were dumb and simple-minded."

"That's true." Joy grins and sighs. "Somewhere along the way, I started to like the fact that I was different. I changed my style, dressed sexy and put on makeup. Suddenly boys were interested in me. And my hair?" She laughs loudly and happily, making my heart skip a beat. "I wanted to bleach my hair blonde, so I put the bleach on the ends to test it. That way, I could cut them off if it failed. They turned green, which I thought that was cool. Green turned blue, then turquoise."

Joy grabs her tips and lifts them up.

"Bleach the tips blonde?" I ask. "Seriously?"

"That's how I got my style," she explains. "How come you didn't recognize me? I recognized you right away."

I'm glad she recognized me after all those years. But I haven't changed that much, we both know that.

"You've changed so much," I confess, "I wasn't sure."

For days, I racked my brain, secretly watching her, but I didn't dare to talk to her. When I finally gathered the courage and found out that she was friends with Sienna, I was shocked. As you might expect, Joy didn't react well to me at all. We're still at that point today.

"Can I explain to you now what made me act the way I did?"

"Hmm."

Joy doesn't seem too thrilled to hear it, but I want to explain it to her anyway.

"I liked you; I liked spending time with you," I tell her, "We had known each other for years and for the first time I saw you as more than Dr. Lin's daughter. I know it's not what she wants to hear, but I want to tell her the truth. Joy avoids my gaze, but I expected that. Of course, she's offended that I never saw her as more than that. The two years that separated us seemed like an eternity then. When I was sixteen, she was just fourteen and still quite childlike. "We got along really well and spent a lot of time together. About halfway through the summer, I found out from my dad that he had a new job in Ohio."

"You knew all along?" she asks, and I sigh.

"Yeah," I answer, wrapping my hands tightly around the porch railing. "I wanted to tell you, but I... I didn't dare. I didn't want to destroy what we had because I was leaving."

"You're crazy." Joy looks at me venomously and keeps shaking her head. "Honestly, you're crazy, Tyler."

"What would have changed if I had told you?" I ask. "You would have pulled away from me and..."

"I wouldn't have slept with you," she hisses. "I would have listened to my gut, saved myself for the right guy and not... not in that boathouse, on... on that couch with you."

I close my eyes for a moment to avoid the disappointment in her eyes. I know it must look like I was just messing with her, but I wasn't. She can't believe that a switch flipped in my head that night and I just wanted to fuck her. That's total bullshit. I would have done it weeks before, but I didn't dare. Precisely because I was always afraid of taking something I wasn't entitled to.

"Do you really think I slept with you on a whim?" I ask. "Jolene... Joy, please. You can't be serious."

"I don't know what I think and what I don't think anymore," she answers, again avoiding my gaze. "The fact that I was in love with you won't take you completely by surprise."

"No."

"Then why did you?" she asks. "You knew I wouldn't reject you."

"Because I was in love with you too."

A silence falls between us and she turns around. She looks at me with wide eyes, and then she starts laughing. Joy isn't just laughing... no, she's laughing at me. She keeps shaking her head like it's the best joke she's ever heard. But damn it, it's not a joke, it's the truth. I was ... am in love with her. She's always been the only one for me. No matter how many I've had sex with, how many times I've come or masturbated. I've always seen her face as she lay there that night, and later her new style replaced that image in my dreams.

"Why are you laughing?" I growl. "Do you find this funny?"

"Sorry." The vixen pretends to wipe a tear from the corner of her eye. "But that's really..."

Furious that she's mocking my feelings, I grab her. Joy yelps as I pin her waist to the porch railing and push myself close enough that she can feel my breath on her face. Her eyes are wide, as if she's genuinely surprised by my behavior. Fuck. She is so incredibly beautiful. I want to kiss her and fuck her against the fucking post to our right, or turn her around, push her over the railing and ... I try to push the thought of her naked ass out of my mind and take a deep breath.

"If I really wanted to deflower you back then and knew I was leaving, I wouldn't have waited until the last evening. Why would I?" I look at her with a grin. "I could have fucked you so many times."

"You..." she hisses and raises her hand to slap me, but I stop her. Instead, I pull her to me and kiss her. "Let me go."

"No," I say. "I want you to understand that I loved you, Jolene."

"Don't call me that."

"Why?"

"You were the only one who called me that, and didn't make me hate the name," she confesses. "I actually liked it."

"Okay."

"Why didn't you tell me?" she asks now. "Let go of my wrist."

"Only if you don't try to hit me again."

"Depends on the answer."

She grins, and I grin back. Then I let go of her wrist. But not without making sure her movements are restricted enough that she can't try again. Freedom of movement is something my cock would really like, too. It's pressing against my jeans and I wouldn't be surprised if she's noticed how hard this is making me.

"I didn't know how to tell you because I knew how disappointed you would be," I tell her. "I kept thinking about it, but in the end I didn't dare. I never intended to sleep with you."

"You're not making it any better."

"What do you want me to say?" I ask. "You don't like the truth, or better yet, you laugh at me. If I tell you something now, you won't believe me either... I fell in love with you back then, Joy. And that evening... in the boathouse... I wanted to kiss you the day before and the day before that, but at the crucial moment, I chickened out."

"I wish you had kept it in your pants that night too."

"You're starting to get on my nerves," I growl. "I can't undo what happened between us. I don't want to. I keep... I keep thinking about that night."

Joy opens her mouth to say something, but at least now she's thinking first and not blurting out the first thing that comes to mind.

"Why didn't you wake me up the next morning ... why did you ... why did you leave me thinking that you just wanted to fuck me?"

It's the first time she doesn't speak to me with anger or condemnation. It's the first statement that reflects her true feelings, and I hate myself for causing them. What if I hadn't moved away? What if we had woken up together that morning? What if I had at least woken her up to explain myself?

"I was afraid of the confrontation," I admit honestly. "I couldn't have looked you in the eye while leaving you."

"Of course, running away is the better option."

"Apparently," I mutter. "I'm so incredibly sorry. I really am. But I don't regret that we slept together and kissed and... and spent the whole summer together. Even if you feel differently."

"I do, yes." Joy looks up at me and takes a deep breath. "Can you please take a step back?"

I do as she asks and let her go. Joy stops, though, and doesn't run away like I expect. Instead, she looks at me, scrutinizing me. I meet her gaze and say nothing. Her lips are pressed together and I want to kiss them to release the tension. But I don't dare. It would destroy everything that has happened between us in the last few minutes.

But then she does something that brings my world to a screeching halt for a moment. Joy walks over to me, puts her left hand on the back of my neck and pulls my head down towards her.

"I'm going to regret this," she murmurs, "but I need to taste you again, touch you again."

I want to ask her what she means and if she's sure, but Joy presses her lips to mine, erasing any rational thought from my mind.

Without hesitation, I grab her around the waist and sit her down on the narrow railing of the porch. Then I slide between her legs and pull her against me. The kiss is passionate, wild and full of unspoken desire for more. We want each other so much it hurts and neither of us knows if what we're doing is right. But I don't care when she unzips my jeans and slides her hand inside.

"Fuck," I gasp. "I wasn't expecting this."

"I know," Joy giggles, biting my lower lip. "Make love to me, Tyler."

I swallow hard and kiss her again. How many times have I imagined this and now it's happening? Joy's hand touches my cock, cupping it, and I moan into her mouth. I shouldn't be fucking her here on the porch railing, but I want her so bad I don't care.

Joy has other plans as she suddenly pulls away and pushes me off her. At first, I think her conscience has kicked in again and she's realized how wrong this is. But that's not what she has in mind. She pulls down my pants and gets on her knees in front of me.

This woman is my undoing and I'm going to enjoy every second of it.

11

Joy

I must have completely lost my mind because I get down on my knees in front of him and pull his jeans down. This evening has taken such an unexpected turn that I don't even recognize myself anymore. I wanted to stay away from Tyler, and after all the incredibly painful memories that have come up in the last half hour, I shouldn't be squatting in front of him and pulling down his pants. But part of me believes him that he saw leaving as the only way to avoid doing more damage. I wouldn't have been happy the next morning if he'd stayed to talk. I probably would have burst into tears and regretted it as much as I regret his subsequent behavior. The difference being that I would have had that embarrassing conversation. Tyler is right, he could have gotten in my pants at any time. Even though I didn't want to hear it, he could have fucked me many more times.

The fact that he was in love with me still leaves me speechless. I didn't want to be disrespectful and laugh, but his confession seemed so unbelievable that I couldn't help it.

I look up at Tyler. He has his eyes closed, waiting patiently to see what I'm going to do next. I'm surprised that he trusts me enough to let me suck him off. I could bite his cock hard enough to make it a painful reminder for days. But no, I don't want to do that. All I want is to exchange that horrible experience with a nice new one. With him. Because like it or not, I can't get away from Tyler Connor.

Tyler takes off his sneakers and jeans. He takes off his socks and looks at me, waiting. I lick my lips with a grin and run my hands down his muscular thighs. Nothing like back then. Nothing about him is like his seventeen-year-old self. I like that.

"Aren't you afraid I'm going to bite your dick?" I want to know and he laughs. Tyler shakes his head and slides his right hand into my hair, gripping it tightly.

"No," he whispers. "You wouldn't do that because you know I wouldn't be able to fuck you then."

"Point taken," I concede, pulling down his boxers. His bulging cock jumps out at me. His head is engorged and the dark red color makes me gasp. I want him so badly. It's been months since I've had the pleasure of sucking off a man. I grab his cock and run my hand up and down. Tyler moans softly. With his head tilted back and his eyes closed, he looks delicious. His hand is loose in my hair.

I place my lips over Tyler's head and slowly slide his shaft into my mouth. He moans with pleasure as I slide it in and out again and again. Tyler is clearly enjoying being pleasured by me and I have to admit that I haven't enjoyed giving a blow job this much in a long time.

"Fuck," he moans. "Stop."

But I don't even think about stopping. I want him to come.

"Jolene." Tyler's grip on my hair tightens and he pulls my

mouth away from his cock. "I want to be inside you when I come."

Excited, I look up at him and lick my lips. Slowly I stand up and grin at him. Tyler looks back at me and pulls me against him. His lips meet mine and I kiss him back. In one smooth motion he takes off my shirt, then his. Then he lifts me in his arms and carries me to the seat on the porch.

Tyler sits me down on his lap and runs his eyes over my face and breasts, which are in a black lace bra. "Have they gotten bigger?" he asks with a grin and plants little kisses on my cleavage. I close my eyes and enjoy the feel of his lips on my heated skin.

I push his face back up so I can look into his eyes. Tyler looks back at me and runs his fingertips down my back. Goose bumps spread across my skin and I press my lips to his. We kiss tenderly, making me forget my plan to just let him fuck me.

"I think they've gotten bigger," Tyler says again, wrapping his hands around my breasts. He massages them and pulls me closer, his cock rubbing through my jeans. "And you're wearing too much."

"Am I?"

Tyler nods. "You are."

I get off his lap and reach around my back to unhook my bra. Slowly, I slide the piece of fabric off my shoulders and toss it on the floor next to me. Then I unbutton my jeans and pull them off as well. My shoes and socks follow until I'm standing in front of him in nothing but my black panties. I don't mind undressing in front of him. Over the last few years, I've learned to like my body and to tone it in all the right places. Judging by the look on Tyler's face, I've done a good job. His eyes scrutinize me as he wraps his hand around his dick to rub it. He looks so hot that I'm getting wetter and wetter. I hook my fingers into the waistband of my panties and pull the last bit of material off my body.

Tyler gulps as I stand naked in front of him.

"Come here!" His voice is raspy - excited - and so am I.

I only slept with him once - my first time. And yet, in the years that followed, I thought of him again and again. We've both had other sexual experiences, and as I climb onto his lap, I realize we're two very different people. We meet at eye level. I'm no longer the shy girl who felt uncomfortable in her skin, and Tyler is no longer the cool guy from high school I idolized. I sit on his lap, put my hands on his shoulders and smile at him.

Tyler's grip on my hips tightens, and as his head brushes against my pussy, we both moan. "We need a condom," he whispers. "There's one in... in my wallet."

I groan in frustration as I pull away from him to get the rubber. For a millisecond, my mind wanders to the blonde from the bar, but I quickly push it away. He wouldn't be here if he'd slept with her.

I go to his jeans and pick them up. Even though I'm on the pill and clean, we shouldn't take any chances. Of course, it's Tyler who thinks about contraception and not me. I take the condom out of his wallet and toss it back on his jeans. As I walk back to him, I open the crackling package and pull out the rubber.

"Do you want to or should I?" I hold the condom out to him, giving him the choice of putting it on himself or letting me do it. Tyler takes the condom from me and wraps it around his cock.

"Okay ... you want to do it yourself," I conclude.

"You talk too much for me." Tyler pulls me onto his lap and positions his dick between us. "I guess you can take me right in."

I raise my eyebrows and want to ask him if he's alluding

to the past. That would be anything but fair, because I didn't know any better. But I don't get the chance. Tyler doesn't give me time to answer and slowly pushes himself into me from below. His bulging cock still stretches me and I moan against his mouth as he pushes himself into me inch by inch. "Fuck," I gasp as he pushes into me all the way. "That's good."

Tyler digs his hands into my hips as well, pressing my body so tight against his that a sheet of paper couldn't fit between us.

"It is," he whispers. "You still feel so perfect."

"Hmm," I sigh. "Perfect."

I start to gyrate my pelvis, and Tyler lets me take the lead. I keep moving up and down, quickening my pace. His hands grip my hips and his lips play around my nipples. He teases them and pulls them deep into his mouth again and again. It feels so good.

"Tyler," I cry out as he slides a hand between our bodies, stimulating my clit as well. "That's it."

God, he knows what he's doing and what I need. We aren't kissing tenderly, nor is the sex. Quite the opposite. Tyler has taken the lead now and drives his cock into me from below. My fingers claw into his shoulders as he suddenly turns us around and lays me on my back on the seat. Tyler puts his right leg on the floor and his left knee on the couch. To penetrate me even deeper, he puts my right leg over his shoulder. I let out a loud moan and put my hand over my mouth. Maybe I should remember that we're not alone out here. But fuck - how can I not moan when he's so good? I throw my head back as he thrusts again.

I realize that Tyler has spoiled me for the rest of the male population - again. He did it emotionally then - now physically.

"Come on, Jolene!" He moans loudly. "Come with me, baby." And I do.

★★★

I'm sitting on our bed in our room and suddenly I feel like I did back then. After we did it on the porch and finally remembered that not only could anyone walk up on us, but that Millie and Darren were in the house, we picked up our things and went inside. This time we didn't jump on each other. Instead, there was an awkward silence, as is often the case when one of you can't just end the one-night stand and leave.

I eventually escaped to the bathroom and took a shower. The few minutes of silence didn't help much, and eventually Tyler asked if everything was okay, and I had to leave my safe hiding place. Then he went into the bathroom.

I can't help but regret what we did. Especially what I started. I kissed him and unzipped his pants first. So much for the idea that it's always the guys thinking about just one thing.

The sex was great, no question, but what happens now? We talked, but we're still stuck in the same place. It would have been smarter to just go to bed after talking and not have sex. Then we would have at least had a small chance of becoming friends. Building a friendship now, after I know how good the sex is with him today, is impossible. Not only did I have fun, but I also felt incredibly comfortable and safe with Tyler. Those aren't necessarily the first qualities I attribute to my one night stand. On the other hand, we'd had sex before. It was no longer a one-night stand.

Annoyed, I groan and run my fingers through my hair.

"Damn it," I curse.

"What's wrong?"

I jump and look at Tyler, completely taken aback. He comes into the bedroom in a fresh pair of boxers and looks at me questioningly. Actually, I've gotten so used to his perfect body over the past few days that at least that doesn't bother me anymore.

"Nothing" I look away. "I'm tired."

"Okay," he mumbles, turning off the overhead light. The small bedside lamp next to me is still on, providing some light. Tyler comes over to the bed and lies down next to me in silence. I smell the spicy scent of his aftershave and want to snuggle up to him. But now we've reached a place I'd hoped to avoid at all costs. Neither of us knows what to say and we're both suffocated by the uncomfortable silence.

The sheet next to me rustles and I don't dare move. Tyler must have turned over. "Joy," I hear him say softly. "Look at me."

I don't answer him. Instead, I stare at the ceiling, hoping he'll forget what he wants to say. Probably not tomorrow or the next day, but eventually it will blow over and maybe we can get back to normal.

"Do you regret it?" he asks the question of all questions and I suck in my breath. No, I don't, but I'm afraid he will. For real this time. I'm afraid that what we shared earlier was just what I want to tell myself: hot sex! But I'm lying to myself. It was much more than hot sex. I don't usually laugh with the guys I sleep with or let them philosophize about my breasts. I have no idea if they've grown, but it's possible. I was only fifteen. No, it was more than good sex with Tyler, and that scares me. He's leaving for the NFL in a few weeks, and our lives will go separate ways again. Maybe not without a goodbye this time, but he'll be leaving me behind again. "I don't regret it."

My heart starts to race. I feel alive again and turn to face him. So close that our noses almost touch. Tyler smiles and gently brushes a strand of hair behind my ear.

"I don't know," I say honestly, barely daring to look at him. "What if... we've complicated everything by doing it?"

"Between us?" Tyler raises his eyebrows in confusion, as if

he doesn't understand my reasoning. "Mostly we fought or ig-nored each other. There wasn't much in between. What could it have complicated?"

"I don't know," I answer, now realizing how illogical my reasoning is. "That was stupid of me."

"It wasn't stupid," he whispers, kissing my forehead. "You're scared, I understand."

"And you obviously aren't." I sound more irritated than I mean to. It strikes me that I'm a nervous wreck and Tyler is taking it in stride.

"Of course, I'm scared too," he replies. "We don't know what's going to happen in Las Vegas in a few weeks, where I'm going to move to ... and you have your own plans. We're at a crossroads again."

"Hm," I mutter and move closer to him. For some mys-terious reason, I need his closeness and Tyler gives it to me. Just like six years ago, he pulls me into his arms. "I can't go to sleep."

"Why?"

"I'm afraid you won't be here in the morning," I blurt out, my heart pounding in my throat.

"That won't happen," he promises me. "At most I'll be in the kitchen listening to Darren's grumbling."

I laugh and look up at him. Through the dim light of the bedside lamp, I can see that he's meeting my gaze.

"I don't understand why he's your best friend."

"Why not?" asks Tyler. "He's the best friend I've ever had."

"I know," I yawn. "Do you mind if I put my legs between yours like this?"

Tyler raises his eyebrows questioningly and doesn't seem to be able to follow my question. This confirms to me that he probably hasn't had a steady partner in the last few years. Otherwise, he would know about this secret weapon. A grin creeps across my face.

"I don't know ..." he says. "Is that good or bad ... for me?"

"Millie, Sienna and Phoe swear that Darren, Denver and Jake can't get up without waking them."

"Okay," he says. "Go for it."

I slide my legs between his and move even closer to him. Maybe a little too close, but tonight I don't care.

"Good night, Tyler."

"Good night, Jolene."

"My name is..."

"Jesus," he growls. "Go to sleep already. I'll always call you that. Good night, baby."

"You really need to work on your nicknames, Bunny."

"Bunny?" Tyler laughs again and his vibrating chest echoes against my cheek. "Good night. Just good night."

"Good night," I agree. "What do you think, darling or honey?"

"Joy, please." He grumbles something I don't understand. "Go to sleep. Now."

Tyler turns off the light and I close my eyes. It doesn't take long before I drift off into a peaceful sleep.

12

Joy

The next morning, scattered sunbeams wake me up, and I blink against their brightness. But they are quickly forgotten as I feel the warm, muscular body pressed against me and the legs entwined with mine.

Tyler! I open my eyes to see his grinning face. "Morning," he mumbles in a sleepy voice. "Sleep well?"

"Like a baby and you?"

"Me too."

There is something soothing about lying in his arms and being held by him. I smile at him and turn to face him. Tyler meets my gaze and brushes back a strand of my hair, exposing my face. My heart races as he makes little circles on my back and leans into me. God, what is wrong with me? I don't know myself or my body like this. I don't like it. My coolness always disappears in Tyler's presence. I immediately put some distance between us.

"I need a shower." I quickly pull away from Tyler because

I don't know how to deal with his closeness. We only had sex, and even though we talked a lot last night, I don't feel like we should be together. His life is going to change completely in a few weeks. I also have plans that I want to follow through with. Right now is the worst possible time to start a future together.

"Okay," Tyler murmurs and lets go of me. He gives me a confused look and sits up in bed. The covers slide down, revealing an excellent view of his torso. He looks gorgeous. Still, I stay strong and don't get back into bed with him. "Do you want coffee?"

"Yeah," I mumble. "Coffee sounds good."

Before the conversation can get any more awkward, I turn and head for the bathroom.

"Joy?" I hear him ask and blink. Please don't say it - please. "Everything is okay between us, right?"

I hear the uncertainty in his voice. He says what I'm asking myself. I don't know if we're okay. Whereas yesterday I was convinced that being honest with him about this 'us' was a good thing, now I disagree. The sex has changed everything.

"Sure," I lie, hoping my voice doesn't sound as pathetic as I feel. "Everything's great."

"Good," he replies and I hear him get out of bed and grab his clothes. "I'll let you take a shower and wait for you downstairs. With coffee."

"Cool," I reply. "Thanks."

Then I disappear into the bathroom as fast as I can and close the door behind me.

★★★

Millie, Darren, Tyler and I went horseback riding today. Darren was especially excited. Things were much better between him and Millie. Tyler and I tiptoed around each other,

114

talking normally, but the underlying lack of communication from this morning hung over us like a dark cloud. We need to talk, and we need to talk soon.

"We're back," I call, sitting down on the seat next to Sadie. Phoenix is seating next to Jake, with Denver and Sienna. "You really have a lovely area around the farm."

"Yeah," Sadie says as Tyler, Darren and Millie join them and sit down. Millie immediately grabs Darren's hand and snuggles up to her boyfriend possessively. Has she still not realized that Sadie is not interested in Darren? And more importantly, Darren is not interested in her!

"You have a lot more pasture than we do in Texas," Darren says. "But the soil is worse."

"We make more money from bull riding, which we prepare the animals for, than we do from actual breeding like you do."

"That's true," he says, pulling Millie even closer. She looks up at him, smiling. I move my eyes to the right and look at Tyler. He looks at me too and smiles briefly. But I don't return it and look away. The baby monitor beeps and Phoenix gets up with a sigh.

"I'll get it," she says to Jake and I use the moment when baby Charlotte needs her mother to escape Tyler's gaze. Besides, I need to talk to someone about what we did. I can't keep it to myself anymore.

Ever since Phoenix returned from Bristol and became a mother, our friendship has suffered. I can't relate to her lifestyle one hundred percent, and I sometimes think I'm too blunt in my responses. She has become very sensitive. Sienna and Millie have a better handle on it. But Phoenix is and always will be my best friend, and I know she feels the same way.

"I'll come with you," I say and stand up as well. Phoenix smiles at me and together we go into the house to check on Charlotte.

115

I can't wait until Sienna and Denver's baby is born. Then we'll have two babies in our group. I'm sure Millie and Darren won't wait long to have a baby either.

Phoenix opens the door to her and Jake's bedroom and it's quiet as a mouse.

"False alarm," she says, grinning at me.

Charlotte is in her crib, her pacifier out of her mouth.

Phoenix pops it back into her mouth and she takes it and sucks on it.

"I slept with Tyler," I blurt out. "Last night and I... I don't know what to do now, Phoe!"

Phoenix's head snaps up and she stares at me, eyes wide. She opens her mouth to say something but closes it again when she realizes she has no off-the-cuff answer. I can see her mind working, trying to come up with something meaningful to say.

"Forget what I said," I retract. "Please just forget it ... it ... it never happened and ..."

"Jolene Lin!" I wince. "Yes, you! How can you just drop the bomb that you slept with Tyler and then not want to talk about it?"

"Because it's not important," I lie, unable to believe that I'm trying to cover it up in front of my best friend. Phoenix sees right through me. "Because... because it... it shouldn't have happened."

Phoenix raises her eyebrows and crosses her arms over her chest. Just like I used to do when we talked about Jake. I wanted it to work out between them and I always told her to keep trying. The way she's looking at me now is the same way I looked at her then.

"That's not unimportant," Phoenix replies. "You've been getting along better since we've been here, haven't you?"

"I have."

"And you're still in love with him?" Her eyebrows rise questioningly, and I press my lips together, not wanting to answer. "Joy."

"Jesus, yes!" I look at her, annoyed. "So, I'm in love with him. But that doesn't change anything."

"Of course it does," Phoenix exclaims, and when I give her a warning look so that everyone on the patio - especially Tyler - doesn't overhear the conversation, she lowers her voice. "You're in love with him and he's in love with you. For me, that's the perfect situation."

"For me, it's just a disaster and a continuation of something that didn't work before, because he has a new phase of his life ahead of him. Without me, mind you."

Phoenix raises her eyebrows and laughs. Then she walks past me. I look after her questioningly.

"Sienna, Millie..." she calls out to the porch.

"What are you doing?" I yell. "Stop it."

"Can you come here, please?"

"Phoenix!" I grab her arm. "Stop it."

"Absolutely not," she replies. "You sit over there."

She points to the couch in the corner. I give her a defiant look and she points again.

"Sit over there," Phoenix says more clearly. "Now we can have a little therapy."

"I don't need any..."

Sienna and Millie appear behind Phoenix, and I roll my eyes. With Phoenix I still had a chance to escape, but against all three of them - no way!

"What's going on?" Sienna wants to know. "We left Sadie alone with the boys."

"Yeah," Millie grumbles. "What's going on?"

"You see, Phoe," I use Millie's really bad mood as an excuse for them to leave. "Sadie's all alone with..."

"Oh no," she cuts me off. "You wouldn't dare use Millie's

jealousy of Sadie as an excuse to avoid your first girlfriend crisis meeting."

I purse my lips and Sienna and Millie's eyes go wide.

"I don't think Darren will get too close," Millie says suddenly. "What's wrong?"

"Can we at least close the door?" I mumble and Phoenix turns around with a grin.

"Is it that serious?" Sienna wants to know and looks at Charlotte who is still sleeping peacefully.

"It is," Phoenix says. "Joy had sex with Tyler."

"Phoenix." I look at her, annoyed. "Not so loud."

"Oh, come on..." She waves it off. "Tyler will seize the moment and let the guys in on it, and..."

"Which is exactly why we should leave it alone," I say. "Don't meddle in it. It won't work anyway."

"Why not?" Sienna asks, giving me an expectant look. "Because he's going to the draft?"

"Yes, and I have my own plans, as you may know, and I'm not going to change them because of Tyler," I snap at my friend, unjustly. They're right. Tyler's and my plans could work together. We still don't know which team will draft him, and I won't graduate for a few months. Everything is still up in the air, and Sienna and Phoenix are facing the same situation. It's clear that both will follow their husbands for the sake of their children. Millie will go with Darren until she gets her inheritance.

Disarmed, I drop onto the couch. Sienna sits down next to me. Phoenix takes Charlotte, who has finally woken up, from her cot and Millie sits on the back of the couch.

"How did you even get to have sex?" Millie asks and I look at her.

"After Tyler had sex with that girl..."

"You mean Sophie?" Phoenix interrupts and I nod. "She's

nice."

"Whatever," I groan. "After Tyler left the bar with Sophie and we had our shots, I left the bar, at some point, with Jake and Phoenix. To my surprise, Tyler was sitting on the patio instead of being with her." I sigh and look at Millie. "I wanted to go to bed, but he said I shouldn't because you and Darren were busy."

"What?" she gasps, blushing as usual. "We were watching a movie."

"Oh, that's what they call it these days," Sienna giggles and Millie rolls her eyes.

"We really did just watch a movie. Then what happened?"

"At first we were having a good time, but then ... then the mood changed." I shake my head briefly, wondering again how it happened. "We started talking about that ridiculous kiss between Sienna and him and ... and then it took on a life of its own. Suddenly it was about our tastes, about Kyle and ... and Sophie, Scott ... oh, I don't know."

I want to get up because sitting like this is driving me crazy, but Sienna stops me.

"Go on," she urges me.

"I ended up telling him he was an asshole." I laugh out loud. "I threw everything at him about back then, and... and it all came flooding back. That he left that he broke my heart, and... and left me alone."

I sniffle and wonder if I'm seriously going to start crying. It can't be. I never wanted to cry about Tyler Connor again. I'd put it behind me.

"Hey," Millie says quietly and sits down on the other side of me. "It's okay."

"After we yelled at each other for a while, he explained himself. For the first time ever, he told me his side of things."

"I take it that was the first time you gave him a chance?"

119

Phoenix asks after putting Charlotte back to bed.

"Maybe," I admit reluctantly. "I never wanted to hear it."

"But now you know ... and what was his reason?"

"He said that everything took on a life of its own that night. He never wanted to sleep with me."

"And then?" Phoenix probes. "Don't make us have to pull every detail out of you, Joy."

"He said he didn't tell me because he didn't want me to break off contact," I continue. "And I might have done that. Then I told him I wouldn't be telling him anything new if I told him I was in love with him, and he... he said..."

I close my eyes for a moment and still can't believe that he was in love with me too and still let it happen.

"He said he was in love with me too."

"We knew it," Sienna exclaims. "Tyler is such a bad actor."

Millie and Phoenix agree with her, of course, and I groan in frustration.

"It helps that you knew," I reply sarcastically.

"Then what happened?" Phoenix doesn't give me a second to catch my breath.

"I laughed at him after he confessed," I continue. "I couldn't believe it and Tyler, he... he didn't find it funny at all."

"And that surprises you?" asks Sienna. "I'm not surprised. How could you be so insensitive?"

"My reaction wasn't the best, I'll admit," I say. "But I didn't know how to handle his confession. Tyler grabbed me and pushed me against the porch railing."

"And then you had sex?" gasps Millie. "Wow."

"Of course not," I hiss. "At least not right away. He said again that he slept with me that night on the spur of the moment. He didn't want to because he didn't want to take advantage of me."

"Do you believe him?" Phoenix asks and I nod.

"Yes, and you?" I look questioningly into the silence. It's important to me what my friends think and if I'm right about my feelings.

"I think so, yeah," Sienna says. "Tyler's not like that. I mean, yes, he has his affairs, but he wasn't trying to take advantage of you at the time. If he wanted to do that, he would have done it weeks earlier."

"He said that too," I reply with a weary smile. "We talked a bit more about the evening and then ... then something in my brain malfunctioned, and I kissed him."

"You kissed him ..." Phoenix gasps. "I didn't expect that."

"Me neither," I agree. "Worse, I told him how much I wanted him and got down on my knees in front of him."

"Joy," Phoenix exclaims almost enthusiastically. "You gave him a blow job without arguing?"

Phoenix knows I'm not into blow jobs. I can totally understand her surprised reaction.

"I did," I sigh. "You can guess the rest."

I look around and my friends say nothing. They look at me in silence, and I'm very grateful that we don't have to talk. Now that I think about it, it's even more amazing that Tyler and I ever got this far.

"It's kind of funny, isn't it?" Millie looks around with a grin. "With us, you can't get enough details, and as soon as you sleep with a guy you care about, you don't tell us anything."

Now that Millie says it, I realize it too. I don't want to talk to them about the sex I had with Tyler because it was special. Because it was wonderful, and I want to keep that moment for both of us. I never realized it, but now that she is confronting me, I realize that I never talked about my first time with Tyler either. I only ever talked about my one night stand.

"I'm sorry," I say, sincerely apologizing to my friends. "I never realized."

"You don't have to apologize," Sienna says, pulling me into a hug. "Every pot has its lid and..."

"Or every pussy has its dick," Phoenix interjects.

"Phoe, please," Sienna cries. "What I'm trying to say is that it's okay that you want to keep this to yourself. It's important to you and it's between you and Tyler. Still, we hope you won't withdraw completely now."

"I won't," I say, unable to resist making another comment. "And before you ask, Tyler eclipses them all."

13

Tyler

After Joy and I had sex last night, I was on an incredible high. At least until this morning when she unexpectedly pulled away and fled to the bathroom. Yes, she fled, there's no other way to put it. When she woke up, I thought everything was fine. I even had a little hope that we had finally taken a step in the right direction after our conversation last night and the sex that followed, but Joy completely withdrew from me. I don't understand why she keeps doing this. She still wants me as much as I want her. But something in her head is so blocked that she can't connect with me.

I take a sip of my beer that Sadie handed me and keep looking into the cabin where Joy and Phoenix first disappeared and then Sienna and Millie a little later. None of them have come back out. I wonder what they're doing in there. Are they cross-examining Joy to find out what happened between us?

But that's ridiculous ... Joy wouldn't do that because she's far too uncomfortable about getting involved with me. On the other hand, they are her friends, and they will know right away that something is wrong. That's a fact. Although we were talking normally most of the time today, I noticed that she was avoiding me. She was visibly uncomfortable being around me or alone with me when Millie and Darren made time to hang out together for a few minutes.

"You're so quiet," Darren whispers to me and I look at him.

"Hm," I reply. "Long day."

"Long day?" He looks at me questioningly. "And this has nothing to do with the girls not coming back?"

"Maybe Phoe, Sienna or Millie have a problem too," I hiss louder than I intend, and Darren looks at me with a broad grin. "You set me up."

I must sound like a toddler who's had his first football taken away and been told he can't play for a week. Not that I'm equating Joy with a football, but I feel a bit like that. I don't understand what the hell her problem is, I thought we'd finally taken a step in the right direction.

"Do you want to talk?" Darren wants to know sympathetically.

"I don't know," I answer and stare into space. "What's the point?"

"It'll make you feel better." My best friend points to the porch railing a few feet away from Denver, Jake and Sadie. "Come on."

Darren stands and looks at me expectantly. Sighing, I stand up and follow him. I don't feel like talking to Darren because it won't change anything. Joy isn't going to suddenly come to her senses, throw her arms around my neck and say she wants to give it a try. I can understand it a bit, but only a bit.

Of course, my life is going to change soon, but that doesn't mean she can't be a part of it and that we can't figure it out. Millie is not going to follow Darren wherever he goes either.

We can have a long-distance relationship, there's nothing wrong with that.

"What happened?" Darren's voice pulls me out of my thoughts, and I look up at him.

"We talked," I tell him. "About the past and about what happened between us. Then she kissed me."

Darren blinks once, then again, then opens his mouth. But he doesn't say anything, which is really rare for him. Obviously, it leaves him as speechless as it does me.

"You're not saying anything."

"She kissed you after you spoke?"

"Yes."

"Just like that?"

"We argued in between, and she laughed at me when I told her I was in love with her at the time."

"She did..." Darren looks at me with wide eyes and takes a sip of his beer. "That's tough. What did you do?"

"I made it clear to her that it wasn't cool," I answer. "She can't just laugh at me when I tell her I was in love with her."

"Am."

"What?"

"You're in love with her," Darren corrects me and I roll my eyes.

"What does that have to do with our conversation right now?"

"Nothing," he replies. "I just wanted to make sure you still are."

"Asshole," I growl. "Are you going to mess with me all night?"

"No," he says. "What happened after that?"

"She laughed at me, like I said, and I grabbed her and pushed her against the porch railing to hold her down so she wouldn't hit me. After another argument, she kissed me. And then the kiss took on a life of its own and we had sex."

I don't tell him that Joy gave me a blow job first, and I don't tell him the exact wording of our conversation, that she literally begged me to do it with her again. I'm not complaining about it. But I know my best friend and his stupid remarks well enough to know that if he had the chance, he would tease Joy about it if given a chance.

"Congratulations, man." Darren slaps me on the shoulder and wiggles his eyebrows. "Now what?"

"I don't know." I turn and lean my butt against the porch railing. I cross my arms over my chest and look at my best friend. "She was acting weird this morning. She wanted to get up and take a shower right away, even though last night..."

I stop myself and shake my head. I can't tell him that either because I know his big, uncontrollable mouth. Millie has tamed him a lot in the last year, but the old Darren still comes out. On the other hand, he's my best friend and how can he give me good advice if I don't tell him everything?

"Last night?" Darren helps me out, as if he knows I have no intention of continuing.

"Last night, after we were in our bedroom, she was weird for a moment, as if she regretted it. But then she got over it and we fell asleep together. She even pulled that ridiculous 'I'll put my legs between yours so you can't get up' thing so I'd still be there the next morning."

"That's rough," Darren says, unable to maintain the seriousness in his voice. "If that's what they want and you go along with it, you're trapped."

"Apparently not," I growl, unintentionally getting louder, causing Denver, Jake and Sadie to glance over at us. That's all I need, Sadie to notice. Joy is going to kill me for talking to Darren. I have to laugh, which makes my best friend look at me strangely. "It's kind of ironic that you're my best friend and she doesn't like you."

"Kind of." He smiles. "How did it go this morning?"

"It was like a switch flipped in her head and she bolted out of bed," I sigh. "The rest of the day, we talked normally, but the awkward situation from this morning lingered between us."

"Until now?"

"Yes," I say, nodding toward the house. "And now she's in there and won't come out so she doesn't have to talk to me."

"Do you want to talk to her?"

"Of course I do," I reply indignantly. "I'm sorry. It just frustrates me that we both want the same thing, but Joy is obviously so afraid that I'm going to dump her again that she won't open up to me."

"Have you ever told her or asked her about it?"

"Of course," I say. "She doesn't want to. But to be fair, I also had to tell her that I have no idea where I'm going after the draft. Still, I told her not to put her plans on hold."

"Which she didn't like either?" Darren speculates and I shake my head.

"Of course she didn't," I answer. "On the other hand, she twists my words—always arranges everything exactly as she needs it in a given situation."

"Do you want me to talk to her?" Darren offers in all seriousness and my eyes widen.

"Absolutely not," I exclaim. "It's nice of you, but ... she'll have a fit. She freaks out when she sees you."

"And that's despite the fact that I never left her alone the next morning." Darren laughs at his joke, but my glare quickly silences him. I don't want to imagine that Joy and Darren ever had a thing. More and more I understand why Denver freaked out when he found out about that stupid kiss. Even though it meant absolutely nothing. "I'm sorry, I didn't mean it that way, honestly."

"I know," I sigh. "I'm acting like Denver."

"What about me?" Denver walks toward us, looking back and forth between us. "Are you okay?"

"Everything's great," I answer.

"So, nothing's great." Denver grins. "What's going on? Something to do with the crisis council in there?"

He nods toward the house, and I roll my eyes.

Why is he asking such a stupid question when he knows?

"Tyler slept with Joy and..."

"Darren," I groan. "What are you doing?"

"He's going to find out anyway, or has this group ever managed to keep anything a secret?" He wiggles his eyebrows. "Not even your canoodling with Sienna..."

"Very thin ice, my friend," Denver grumbles. "Do you really have to bring that up all the time? Can't we just use the fact that Jake got my little sister pregnant as an example?"

"If you tell us which one of us had his dick in Phoe at the same time so that he could also be considered a father and make Jake jealous - yes! If not - no!"

I have to laugh briefly at Darren's example and then scowl at him.

"It might have been the first time it wasn't 'discussed' in the group," I reply annoyed. "Thanks."

"Anytime," Darren replies cheerfully, grinning at me. "Joy will calm down again. It worked with Millie, Sienna and Phoenix."

"Oh, and how long will that take?" I want to know from this wise guy.

"You didn't see each other for six years after the first time" Denver joins the conversation again. "Actually, Darren's six days with Millie were too much."

"It was only four days," Darren corrects him unnecessarily.

Annoyed, I shake my head and walk past them back to our table to sit down again. Jake looks at me questioningly, but I don't react. I don't want to discuss it in front of Sadie. Phoenix or Denver, if not Sienna, will let Jake know soon enough. I can't believe that only one of them doesn't know. I bet they've known I had been with Joy since I got here and never said anything, the bastards.

"I'm going to go check on the girls," Sadie says suddenly, getting up quickly. I knew she would figure it out. We weren't particularly smart when we only moved two steps away and then Denver joined us.

"I'm glad Sadie knows too."

"After the way you keep giving her brother's death stares, she was bound to figure out that there's more going on between you and Joy," Jake says.

I groan and lean back. Of course, it hasn't gone unnoticed by Sadie, but maybe her going into the house will make the girls come out. Sure enough, Millie and Sienna come out onto the porch soon after.

"I'm tired," Sienna announces, putting her hand on her stomach. So far it is not obvious that she is pregnant. When Phoenix returned from Europe, she was seven months pregnant and couldn't hide her baby bump. Sienna, on the other hand, is still slim and trim. Her pregnancy isn't going to show much.

Denver stands and pulls his girlfriend close to him. He looks at her with a smile and plants a soft kiss on her lips. "Let's go to bed," he says, saying good night.

"Sleep well and see you tomorrow."

"See you tomorrow," Darren, Millie and I say in unison.

"Are we going to bed too?" Darren wants to know and looks at Millie with a grin. I roll my eyes in exasperation. They can't want to have sex again, can they?

"We didn't have sex last night," Millie says suddenly, and I turn around. "We just watched a movie and fell asleep."

"Oh!"

"Don't worry about it." Darren looks at me and then at Millie as a dirty grin appears on his lips. "We don't plan on making a habit of it."

"You mean like tonight?" I wonder.

"That too." Millie slaps his chest. "Ouch! What was that for?"

"That was for always blurting things out. It's none of Tyler's business."

I have to agree with her, it's none of my business and I don't want to know as long as I'm in this mess with Joy. It's not particularly nice knowing that everyone around you has a great sex life except you.

"And sometimes Tyler doesn't even want to know," I answer.

"Sometimes?" Millie raises her eyebrows.

"Always," I correct myself and wink at her. "I never want to know."

"That's better," she replies, looking at her partner. I look away and pick up the empty bottles as Phoenix and Joy come out of the house. Sadie follows them.

"Good night," Joy says, not looking at anyone, and leaves the porch in the direction of our cabin. I stand rooted to the spot, bottles in hand, watching her go. What's going on now? She could at least wait until we're done.

"Go after her," Phoenix hisses at me. "Now."

"Why?" I want to know and immediately get a slap on the back of my head. "Why are you hitting me?"

"Because you're stupid." Phoenix snatches the bottles from me and points in the direction that Joy disappeared. "I'm sure Millie and Darren will be happy to stay with us for a while."

"I..." I try to justify myself.

"Move, Tyler, or you'll get to know me," Phoenix snaps at me, making me jump. "You broke her heart once and if you do it again, I swear I'll rip your balls..."

"What Phoenix means is," Jake saves me by covering her mouth. "We've got your back so you can fix it."

"No, that's not what I was saying." Phoenix has pushed Jake's hand away from her mouth. "I was saying I'll rip your balls off and your dick too if you hurt her again."

"I get it," I reply, raising my hands disarmingly. "I don't intend on hurting her again, but I'm not her punching bag either. Her mood swings regarding this matter are annoying. Speaking of mood swings..." I raise an eyebrow. "Are you pregnant again?"

"Get lost, Tyler."

Laughing, I look at Phoenix again and follow Joy to our vacation home.

14

Joy

I hear the crunch of gravel behind me and sigh.

"Hey." Tyler comes up next to me and smiles at me. "You okay?"

I look up at him slowly and shrug. I wish he hadn't followed me to ask if I was okay. Talking to the girls didn't make me feel any more certain about him... about us. I feel even more unsure that what I want is wrong and that I'm on the verge of losing him again.

"Sure," I answer, crossing my arms over my chest, "how about you?"

"Same." I have no idea whether he's telling the truth or not. Honestly, I don't want to know because I don't feel the same. "Want to watch another movie?"

I look up at him and shake my head. Watching a movie is a bad idea. Watching a movie is like having coffee. It's a code word for sex, and sex is the last thing Tyler and I should be having right now. Although the sex with him was really, really good. I wouldn't mind doing it again, but not with him. It's not going to work if we are separated by distance.

"No," I answer and see his shoulders slump. Did he seriously expect a different answer? "I'm tired. I want to go to bed."

"More like avoiding me," he mutters, but I hear him perfectly.

"So what," I retort. "It's my business."

Tyler stops and I'm about to move on when he grabs my wrist and pulls me back. I slam into his chest and look up. His blue eyes search mine and it doesn't take a second before his right hand is on my cheek and his left hand is on my hip, pulling me closer to him. My heart starts beating faster and my heart rate spikes as this outrageously hot guy slides his hand under my shirt to touch my bare skin. His fingertips make little circles on my hips.

"Stop that," I make a feeble attempt to push him away. "Please."

Oh wow, not only do I sound desperate, I sound scared. What is wrong with me? I don't recognize myself like this, and I don't like it. Never before has a guy managed to intimidate me and make me doubt my own decisions like Tyler.

"Why are you avoiding me?" he wants to know impatiently. His jaw clenches and I can tell it's taking all his control not to freak out. "Why don't you give me a chance to get it right this time?"

"I can't," I say. "Tyler, please, I... I can't do this. I ... I have plans and..."

"What's wrong with us making plans together?"

"Because we're not doing it," I snap at him, pushing him away. Surprisingly, he's caught off guard by my outburst, and I break free. "Your life path has been predetermined since... since high school? I don't know, Tyler. You want to go to the

134

NFL, but the NFL doesn't ask about your preferred city, it doesn't ask if you've settled in and if you like your team. And you know that! I don't want to live out of a suitcase for the next ten or even twenty years because you have to move from one team to the next."

He swallows hard and closes his eyes. Then he shakes his head, and it takes a moment before he opens them again and looks at me. His beautiful blue irises scrutinize me. They look tortured, as if he has finally realized that we will never come to an agreement.

"Would you be willing to try if I became a lawyer or ... or an economist? Is it all about the draft dictating my future and then the NFL?"

I look at him for a moment and think. I really don't know. Of course, it would be easier if he knew what his future looked like. Then we could decide together. Not the National Football League, a club somewhere in the country, or just a big check from the franchise.

But who's to say he'd come to California with me if that were the case? I want to go to Los Angeles and work as a psychologist. That's my dream, and I've been working toward it since I started college in Lincoln. I don't want to have to put my dreams on hold now because my boyfriend has to travel around the country and has an uncertain future from year to year.

"It doesn't matter," I dodge his question. "I have plans."

"It does matter," he growls. "What if I get drafted by a team in California? San Francisco or Los Angeles? Even Las Vegas is doable by car or in an hour by plane. What excuse will you have then?"

The word 'excuse' rings in my ears. Are these excuses I'm giving him, flimsy reasons not to give him a chance? I purse my lips and look at him.

135

"They're not excuses," I hiss. "Stop mocking me."

"I'm not mocking you," he retorts, putting his hands on his hips. Tyler's patience with me is wearing thin. I can even understand it to some extent because no matter what he says or suggests, I dash his hopes within seconds. "I just can't follow your reasoning. You say you don't want me because of the NFL, but I have to find a club first before it's an issue. What's your second argument? That I'll leave again? That won't happen, I'm not that stupid anymore.

My heart skips a beat. He's not going to leave me hanging again and not contact me for six years, but there's still this little voice in my head warning me against him. Telling me that this is all a bad idea. All the independence I've fought for these past years will be gone if I get involved with Tyler. He and his career will control my life going forward. The city I live in, the people I associate with - even where I work if it could tarnish his image. If I even went to work. What would be the point of taking a job if I had to move every year?

"Jolene," he sighs and walks toward me. Just the sound of my full name makes my skin tingle. I don't back away this time, waiting to see what he does next. Tyler cups my face with his hands and pulls me towards him. "I can't do more than tell you that I want to try. Damn it, I... I've only ever wanted you."

My heart stops and my eyes widen. He's only ever wanted me? That can't be true, I don't believe it. Tyler is two years older than me. He's had a lot of girls before and after me. It's unbelievable that he would choose me.

"You have..." I shake my head. "That can't be true. Why?"

"Why?" Tyler laughs and takes another step towards me. His hands slide from my cheeks to the back of my neck so he can angle my head. The bastard knows exactly how to keep me from moving away from him. "I don't know, but I couldn't get you out of my mind. I'm not going to lie to you and tell you

136

that there was no one after you. That wasn't the case."

It's true, but I still don't want to hear it. No matter how silly it sounds, I don't like the idea of him being with other women. It makes me incredibly uncomfortable, and I want to tell them all that Tyler is mine. It's just so weird to me. I've had a lot of sex in the last few years, I've had a steady relationship with Anthony, and I've fooled around. I don't know if he's had a steady relationship, but I don't think so.

"No," I say. "It wasn't like that."

"Did you have a relationship?" he asks. "After we..."

He doesn't finish the sentence, but I know what he means.

"I had a steady boyfriend," I answer, feeling Tyler's body tense. He wanted to talk about it, not me. To my astonishment, he lets go of me and pulls away. An incredible coldness surrounds me, as if I've pushed him away with my confession. I cross my arms over my chest to protect myself from the negative feelings. "His name was Anthony. I met him a few weeks after you left."

"How long were you together?" There's hardly any expression on Tyler's face. His gaze is distant and cold, as if I'm telling him his career is over.

"Almost three years, until we went to college," I answer. "We wanted to start this new phase of our lives unattached. It wouldn't have worked out. But that was okay. I didn't have a steady boyfriend in college."

The corners of Tyler's mouth quirk up and he smiles. I hope he doesn't think I've been living chastely like the Virgin Mary ever since. Because I haven't. I actually had a very fulfilling sex life until he showed up in Lincoln and turned everything upside down. After that, I went on some dates, had a few one-night stands, but Tyler was a constant presence in my dirty thoughts.

"And you?" I ask. "Did you have a steady girlfriend?"

"No," he says. "It was always just sports for me. A steady girlfriend and football don't always go well together."

Now I can't help but laugh out loud. He's scored an own goal with that statement, and what an own goal it is! For days, he's been trying to convince me to ditch my doubts about his lifestyle, and now he says something like this.

"You're trying to convince me to throw my doubts about your lifestyle to the wind, and you say something like that?" I continue to laugh. "Way to go, Tyler."

He groans and rolls his eyes.

"Twist my words all you want," he sighs. "I get it, life with me is probably not like life with an office guy."

"Definitely not."

"But it has a lot of advantages."

"Oh yeah?" The corners of my mouth turn up in a cheeky grin and his eyes flash. "Like what?"

"Well," he begins, closing the distance between us. "First of all, suits fit me better because I have a damn good body."

"A matter of opinion." I try to sound disinterested and cool, but he knows that's more pretense than reality. Of course, with his six-pack abs, broad shoulders, and chiseled arms and legs, he looks terrific in a suit.

"I'm offering you a more exciting life," he continues. "You can travel with me to the most remote destinations and the most beautiful beaches."

"My office guy can save up for that."

Tyler rolls his eyes.

"I fuck better."

"Your arguments are lame and totally outdated," I say, but I can't help smiling. "Maybe I don't want a guy who's good at fucking, I want a guy who's around."

"I'm here," he replies. "And I know what you want and what you need. That includes good sex."

"Like I said..." I make a sweeping gesture with my hand. "I don't want a guy who fucks well, I want a guy who's there for me."

"Joy," he sighs and takes my hands, pulling me against his chest. "You're trying to discredit or diminish every argument I make to tell me that you don't want me. If I were an office guy, you'd come up with other arguments; if I were a doctor or a firefighter, you'd come up with different ones. It's ridiculous."

He plants a kiss on my forehead and lingers. I take a deep breath, enjoying the feel of his soft lips on my skin way too much. Then he lets go of me and takes a step back. I look at him. Tyler hesitates for a moment as if to say something, but he doesn't. Instead, he steps back and starts walking towards the house.

I've accomplished my goal now, haven't I? Tyler has realized that I don't want him. I should be happy, but the pain in my stomach tells a different story. On the contrary, I feel awful.

15

Joy

I twirl my beer glass in my hand and can't take my eyes off Tyler and Sophie. They're sitting at the next table with Sadie, Jake and Phoenix. She moves closer to him every minute and I can't believe he doesn't seem to mind. Tyler responds to her ridiculous attempts to get close to him. He laughs at her jokes and keeps giving her flirtatious looks.

He's been avoiding me ever since we discussed the future outside our cabin the day before yesterday and I made it clear to him again that I couldn't see a future with him. It was exactly what I wanted, but now I'm not happy about it either. It hurts to see him with someone else. Especially since he's been with her before. Different place, different situation, but they still left together. The more I see them together, the less I believe that there was nothing between them back then. Back then, how ridiculous that sounds. As if it was months or years ago. But it hasn't even been a week.

Sophie is pretty, no question, and I even understand why

141

Tyler likes that she's hitting on him. Looking at her, I don't think I'm his type. It's ridiculous. Sophie is exactly the same type of woman as Sienna, and he already stuck his tongue down her throat.

"It might help if you only looked half as murderous." Sienna slides into view with a smirk and I roll my eyes. I don't care what my expression looks like. I want Sophie to know that I don't like her buzzing around Tyler like a mosquito. "Just a suggestion."

"Leave me alone," I grumble, avoiding my friend's gaze.

I don't mean to be so hostile towards Sienna, but this whole thing with Tyler is getting to me a lot more than I thought. First, he tries to convince me that he's the one and then he shows no interest. It just doesn't add up.

"Leaving you alone is not an option." She grins at me and sits down on the free barstool next to me. "What happened to make you two so... well... distant?"

"Her!" I point at Sophie. "She throws herself at him all the time."

"All the time?" Sienna looks at Sophie and Tyler and then back at me. She shakes her head and sighs. "They get along, but that's it. You're as paranoid as Millie."

"I'm not..." I can't believe Sienna is siding with her. "They've disappeared together before, may I remind you."

"You may, and what happened between them?"

"Nothing," I admit meekly, looking past Sienna to Sophie and Tyler. "At least that's what Tyler said, but he'll say anything to get in my pants."

Sophie's left hand is on his upper arm, and I could swear she'd like to slide it even farther up his bicep, under the hem of his shirt.

"And why do you think something's going to happen today?" Sienna asks, raising her eyebrows.

She's right. There's no clear indication that something is happening between them. Tyler isn't even responding to her advances. He's chatting with Jake.

"Are you blind?" My response is ridiculous, and the way Sienna looks at me, she thinks so too. Still, I don't want to imagine the two of them in bed together.

"I'm not blind," my friend explains with a grin and a wink. "All I see is Sophie touching his arm and Tyler ignoring it. There's nothing in his body language that says he wants to have sex with her. And you know it."

"Hmm."

"Joy," Sienna sighs. "Look at me."

I turn away from Sophie and Tyler so I can look at Sienna. My friend has a smile on her face. One of those smiles that makes it clear that she knows I'm making a fool of myself. I'm jealous of Sophie because she's where I want to be - at his side.

"I know what it's like," she explains, "when Denver and I were just starting out and most girls didn't think it was serious..." Sienna shakes her head, as if recalling unpleasant memories. But that's ridiculous. Denver has only had eyes for her since the first time they met. "You have to trust Tyler and believe he's serious."

"Then why has he been avoiding me for two days?"

"Maybe because you've made it clear to him several times that you don't want to be part of his life?" Sienna shakes her head in disbelief. "His path is set, and I'm sure he would do anything to influence the draft, but he can't. No one can, not even Millie. Tyler would never force you to go with him if you were happy on the other side of the country."

"You say that like it's all my fault."

"Isn't it?" Sienna's eyebrows shoot up and I groan. "Talk to him and I bet it will all work out."

"And if it doesn't?" I ask cautiously, looking back at Tyler and Sophie. He has now turned his attention from Jake to her. I grip my glass tighter, barely able to control the green-eyed monster inside me. What the hell is this feeling? I always thought Millie was exaggerating about Darren, but maybe she wasn't. I also don't trust these blond Australians anymore.

"I'd love to have a drink with you." Sienna pulls me out of my thoughts, and I look at her. "At least then Denver's snoring would be more bearable tonight." She shakes her head and I can't help but laugh. "Don't laugh," she sighs. "He can knock down an entire forest with that snoring."

"I'll drink for both of us and pass it telepathically to you," I suggest with a grin. "All without harming the baby."

"Telepathy?" Sienna laughs. "We can try it sometime."

Sienna and I walk over to Darren, Kyle and Denver's table. There's a bottle of tequila and glasses in the middle of the table. I stand between Denver and Darren. Kyle is across from me with Sienna.

"Hi, baby," Denver purrs. He puts his arm around her waist and gently strokes her belly. "Are you okay?"

"Everything's fine," Sienna answers with a grin and nestles against him. I let my gaze linger on them for a moment. I've never been jealous of my friends because they're in a relationship. Why would I be? I genuinely wish them the best, but more and more I feel like I want more, that what they have is exactly what I want. Unfortunately, with the wrong guy.

"Do you want a drink?" Darren asks and I nod.

He pours a drink for all of us and sets a glass of water down for Sienna.

"I'll have one too." Sadie joins us and smiles at Darren. "Please."

"Sure," he replies and pours her a glass.

"Where's Millie?" I ask more suspiciously than I'd like, looking at Darren. He shrugs and turns back to Sadie.

144

Annoyed that he doesn't answer me, I grab his arm and force him to look at me. His jaw is clenched and there are flashes of lightning in his eyes that could make me drop dead. "Where's your girlfriend?"

I emphasize the word girlfriend.

"My girlfriend," he growls, "is wherever. Okay? I have no idea, and before you ask any again... I don't care."

"You don't..." I falter, and Sienna gasps in surprise. "Where's Millie?"

"Leave me alone and mind your own business," he snaps. "I've got enough to deal with, and I really wonder what Tyler sees in you."

I gasp and look at Darren with a mixture of anger and confusion. I don't like this jab. I don't want Tyler discussing us with Darren. It already bothers me that he's his best friend and knows everything.

"It's a good thing that it's Tyler's decision."

"Not if I can talk him out of it." Darren really doesn't seem to have any qualms about telling me to my face that he wants someone else for Tyler.

"Stop it." Sienna pulls away from Denver and stands between Darren and me. "Seriously, Darren." She raises her eyebrows. "Where's Millie?"

He sighs and runs his fingers through his hair.

"I really don't know," he confesses, and now I can see the concern for his girlfriend in his eyes. Darren always acts like he's the toughest player on the field - in life or on the field - but when it comes to Millie, he turns into a worried little kitten. "We had a fight - again - and I told her to do what she had to do and left."

"Great," I sigh. "Was it because of her?" I nod and point at Sadie.

"Me?" Sadie points at herself. "I've said it before and I'll

145

say it again: I don't want anything from Darren. We get along well, and if Millie can't stand to be around women other than her best friends who get along with him and have things in common, maybe she should get some help."

"Watch your mouth," I hiss, about to take a step forward when Sienna stops me. Her hand grips my upper arm and her look clearly tells me not to do anything rash. "Let's go see where she is," she says, "and you should think about what you want, Darren."

"Fuck you, Sienna."

"Hey!" Denver appears behind us. "Don't talk to her like that."

"Sorry," he mumbles, shaking his head. "I didn't mean it."

I give him one last withering look, then walk past him to leave the bar and find Millie. I can't believe he just left her there.

Sienna and I step outside and see Millie sitting on the sidewalk across from the entrance.

"Hey," Sienna says, and she looks up. "We were looking for you."

Millie shrugs.

"You think I'm overreacting?" she asks. "I ... I really tried, but she..." Millie throws her hands in the air. "She's always with him. We've been arguing ever since we got here."

Sienna and I sit down on either side of her. Millie is dejected and I feel incredibly sorry to see her like this. Darren is such a complete idiot that he can't see how bad his girlfriend is feeling because of his flirting.

"Seems like an Australian thing to do," I grumble and Sienna gives me a questioning look. I'm sure that's not what Millie wants to hear right now, but I need to vent a little too. Sophie is stuck to Tyler like glue.

"What do you mean?" Millie looks at me questioningly. If I

tell her about Tyler and Sophie, it will only reinforce her suspicions about Sadie, and I don't want that.

"It doesn't matter." I wave her off. "Darren's a jerk, but…"

"Joy," Sienna scolds. "Can you say it without insulting him?"

"No," I answer sweetly. I even elicit a small laugh from Millie with my answer. "Darren loves you."

"Wow." Millie shakes her head and laughs. Her response is the bitchiest I've ever heard her. Normally she's always nice and tries to keep her temper in check. Darren's bad behavior and our blunt way of saying things are starting to rub off on her. "I haven't noticed much of that."

"Seriously?" I raise my eyebrows. "He's been following you around for a year, like a puppy following its mother."

"And the puppy will eventually leave its mother," she replies grimly, staring at the entrance to the bar.

I roll my eyes and look at Sienna.

"How's it going with Tyler?" Millie looks at me and I realize that the change of subject is much too easy for her. Even though I don't want to talk about him, I'm helping a friend.

"He's attached to Sophie."

"So, that's what you meant by 'Australian style'?"

"Yes," I say, also staring at the entrance to the bar, hoping that Tyler will come out and tell me there's been a misunderstanding about Sophie. But that's not going to happen. I think I pushed him away for good with my reaction the day before yesterday. "He wanted a second chance," I tell them. "The day before yesterday … and … and give it a try until the draft. After that, I'm supposed to decide whether to go with him or do my own thing."

"And you turned him down?" Millie asks cautiously. I nod. "And now he's probably tired of trying to convince you."

"Apparently," I mutter. "It's probably for the best. I don't want that life ... I want my place, my home and ... and I don't want to move anymore."

"Isn't our place with them?" Sienna looks at me and raises her eyebrows. "For me, it was clear that my place was with Denver. Even before the pregnancy. The baby is another big reason to go with him, but I think the most important reason of all is..." She stops herself and takes a deep breath. "I love Denver. It doesn't matter if we live in New York, Chicago or Los Angeles, and it doesn't matter how long we're there."

"Why doesn't it matter to you?" I ask, genuinely interested. "I knew from the beginning of my studies that I wanted to live and work as a psychologist in Los Angeles. I don't want to throw my plans out the window and ... and possibly have to move every few years. That's not the life I want for myself."

"It is more important for me to be with Denver," says Sienna, "Yes, we will have to put up with a lot, adapt, and possibly move several times in the next ten to twenty years. We have no idea how long he'll play. But we will be together and soon to be a family."

Sienna's speech really affects me. Of course, we'd have to deal with all that, but she's right, we'll have each other and make new friends in our respective cities. Once we have kids - which Tyler and I are light years away from, thank God - it won't matter what we want personally anyway.

"So did I overreact and hurt him?" I ask my friends candidly. I feel uneasy inside because I don't want to hear their answers. Because I already know them. Tyler is just asking for a chance, and I keep looking for reasons not to give it to him. Maybe he's right and a team from California will draft him. Maybe not Los Angeles, but San Francisco, Las Vegas or San Diego - all close to my dream city.

"Well..." Millie tries to sugarcoat it.

"Yes, you did." Sienna looks at me triumphantly. "And

you're jealous of Sophie, which I can understand, because unlike Sadie, she really is hitting on Tyler."

"You're just telling me this now?" I growl, a knot forming in my stomach. I don't want to think about Tyler having sex with Sophie. I don't want that scenario in my head.

"Of course I'm telling you now." Sienna laughs and flips her blonde hair back. Her eyes sparkle at me. Then she points at Millie. "Because unlike Millie, you show it nonverbally."

"I'm so stupid."

I ruffle my hair and stare at the asphalt beneath me. Tyler is right. If I don't give him - us - a chance, we'll never find out if it will work. And we should find out, preferably before he goes to the draft, and his future is decided.

"Millie?" I ask and she looks at me. "Are you going with Darren? I mean ... unlike us, you already have your position in life. Until then ... will you go with him?"

"Sure," she answers without hesitation. The sparkle in her eyes shows me how much she loves him and how natural it is for her. "It will be years before I officially accept my inheritance. And as Sienna says, my home is where Darren is. Besides, I have enough money to fly across the country to see my best friends."

If they can do it, so can I.

16

Tyler

Here's the thing about one-night stands: They're a one-time thing.

Why the hell don't women understand that? Annoyed, I sip my beer and shake off Sophie's arm for the umpteenth time. It was a stupid, stupid mistake to fuck her. I thought she wanted a distraction from Kyle or Scott and I wanted a distraction from Joy when I fucked her in the alley behind the bar. It was a quick thing. Pants down, skirt up, condom on, done. But now she's clinging to me like I put a ring on her finger. It sucks and it's even worse because Joy has been watching us the whole time, thinking I'm interested in her. I'm not. I was so sure that Sophie was secretly into Kyle. I had ruled out Scott because he's a few years older than her.

"I'm going to see Darren," I say, turning around with my beer in my hand before Jake can react. It's not nice to leave him alone with Phoenix and Sophie, but I can't stand being around her anymore. The little hearts that flash in her eyes

151

when she looks at me make me want to puke. I hate it when girls start gushing because you satisfied them once.

The only one who would never do that is Joy. She would never in her life look at me like that or make me feel like I'm the greatest guy in the world. To her, I'm just me - Tyler. And I like that. Unfortunately, Ms. Lin keeps making it clear that she will sabotage anything that has to do with me and a future together. She's strictly against us living together, even if it's just to see if we're compatible over the next few weeks. Which, in my opinion, we are, without a doubt.

I step next to Darren and point to the tequila in the middle. "Me too."

My best friend furrows his eyebrows in concern, but I give him a look that lets him know I don't want to talk about it right now. Not everyone in this bar needs to know that things aren't working out with Joy. Not to mention her endless excuses for why we can't be together. That's why I walked out on her the day before yesterday. I've tried to convince her over and over again, but I just don't know what to do anymore. Now it's definitely up to her if she wants to be with me and give us a chance at a future together.

"Here." Darren puts the tequila down for me and pours himself a generous shot. "To us."

"To us," I agree, swallowing the alcohol without the salt and lemon. It burns my throat terribly, but that doesn't seem to stop Darren from pouring more right away.

"Where's Millie?" I ask, looking around the bar for her.

"Offended."

My eyebrows shoot up and Darren groans.

"She's outside or at our place," he grumbles. "I don't know, okay?"

"Did you two have another fight?" I ask, scrutinizing him closely. Darren's usually cool demeanor slips a bit and he

152

grinds his teeth as he nods. "Why this time?"

Without saying anything, he jerks his head in Sadie's direction, and I groan in annoyance. This can't be happening. I thought they'd finally sorted things out and moved on. Looks like they haven't.

"Darren," I sigh and massage the bridge of my nose, hoping to come up with something useful to say. But honestly, he and Millie are beyond help. She's jealous for no reason, but he doesn't give her the reassurance that her jealousy is unfounded. He spends too much time with Sadie. "Come with me."

I grab my best friend's arm and pull him out of the bar and onto the porch behind us. Once there, he leans his butt against the railing and crosses his arms over his chest like a toddler. For God's sake, I'm not his mother giving him a moral lecture.

"Don't be so childish," I say. "I'm not your mother."

"I could use her here, too." He rolls his eyes, and I could swear he trembled for a second. "What do you want to tell me, Ty? You're struggling with Joy, and fucked Sophie."

"You fucked her?" My heart drops into my pants and I spin around. Millie, Sienna and Joy are standing on the porch steps looking at me in stunned silence. Joy is white as a sheet and starting to shake. Fuck, fuck, fuck. She was never supposed to know that I had sex with Sophie.

I can't utter a sound and instead look at Darren, who looks at me apologetically but has nothing to say in his defense. What can he say? He told Joy that I had sex with Sophie.

"What are you all doing out here?" Sophie is standing in front of us, followed by Sadie and Phoenix. "Is everything okay?"

I look at them and then at Joy. She looks back at me, turns on her heel and disappears.

"Joy!" Millie turns back to us on the stairs. "And you're sleeping on the couch tonight."

153

Darren turns and stares at his girl.

"Oh, and why is that?" he yells. "What's your fucking problem?"

"My..." Millie swallows, tears forming in her eyes. "You know what it is."

"No, I don't," he shouts. "I .... I just want us to have a good time and... and you're just stressing me out."

"Darren," Sienna says, giving him a warning look. "Not here."

She's right, they really don't need to discuss it here. Especially not in front of Sadie. It's none of her business. I continue to believe that she's not interested in him and only likes him. The problems between Darren and Millie go much deeper than Sadie's friendship with Darren.

"Fuck you," Millie hisses and follows Joy.

Darren throws his hands in the air and kicks the chair to our left. "Fuck," he shouts.

"What's going on?" Phoenix squeezes between Sophie and Sadie.

"Your friends are gone," I say. "I'm going to check on Joy."

"And I'll check on Millie."

Darren follows me.

★★★

Joy and Millie have vanished off the face of the earth. We looked all around the bar and then went to the house. But we didn't find them on the mile-long walk here nor in the house. Now we're sitting on the porch in silence.

"Millie can't conceive naturally."

Darren speaks so softly that I think I've misheard him. The despair in his eyes and his slumped shoulders speak volumes. We sit across from each other, but Darren doesn't look at me.

154

His forearms rest on his thighs and he keeps running his hands through his hair as if searching for a solution. But I know there's no solution. I find it difficult to utter a word. I can only imagine what it must be doing to Millie and their relationship. She's a real family person, and unlike Darren, she has a very good relationship with her family.

"How long have you known?"

"Since we got here," he answers quietly. "She got a call from her gynecologist that first morning."

Darren lifts his head and quickly wipes his eyes. But I've already seen that they're moist.

"Millie can't handle it at all, and I... I'm sure she hasn't told the girls either."

"Do you think it's because of Sienna's pregnancy?"

"Yes," he says. "She doesn't want it to affect the way Sienna deals with her pregnancy. That's so typical of her..." He ruffles his hair. "She's miserable and all she cares about is not making Sienna feel bad. I don't give a damn if Sienna thinks twice about putting the damn ultrasound on the table or not."

I want to tell him that he's being unfair to Sienna. She's very sensitive and if she knew, she would never do that. She would be considerate of Millie and Darren. Denver as well. But I'll address that when things have settled down and Darren is better able to deal with the whole situation. It's no less devastating for him than it is for his girlfriend.

"Why didn't you leave?" I ask. "It's not good for you to be here. Now her jealousy of Sadie makes a lot more sense."

"She doesn't want to." Darren sighs heavily and wipes his eyes again. "I'm sorry, man."

"Are you seriously going to apologize for that right now?" I growl. "Damn it, Darren! You're never going to be able to have kids. At least not naturally. You can't just brush that off."

He shouldn't be embarrassed about being upset. I'm glad

he confided in me. Maybe it's time he talked about it. It would do him good to talk about it. Even if I don't think I can give him any good advice. I don't have children myself, or even a friend in the same situation.

"How did it even come up?" I ask cautiously. "I can't imagine Millie specifically had herself tested for it?"

"No," says Darren. "It was more of a coincidence. She was at her gynecologist wanting to switch from the pill to the IUD. She always had a very strong reaction to the pill. We discussed it because we wanted to sleep together without using a condom, but she needed a different kind of birth control. Millie took a hormone test as a precaution, and the results were devastating.

"I'm... I'm so sorry." My stuttering doesn't help Darren either. "For both of you."

"Thank you," Darren whispers, kneading his hands together. "Kids weren't really on my mind for the next ten years. Millie's going to take over the Minneapolis Warriors, and I'm going to play. There's no time for kids, and we both knew that. But now everything looks different. For her, it's devastating. Her first question was if I wanted to stay with her under these circumstances. Millie believes I'm going to leave her sooner or later because of this."

"Which you won't."

"Of course I won't," he snaps at me, clenching his hands into fists. "She's my dream girl. I love her more than anything. And if it's just the two of us, then so be it. Besides, we have enough money to explore other options. She knows that too, but at the moment she's completely closed to the subject."

"I'm your dream girl?" An incredibly thin and shy voice interrupts our conversation, and we look up. Darren immediately jumps up and rushes over to Millie, who throws herself into his arms without hesitation. "I'm so sorry," she sobs, "I've been so freaked out since... since I found out."

"I understand, baby," he says, stroking her back. Darren pulls away from Millie and looks into her eyes. He gently brushes away her tears and kisses her. "But I love you more than anything. I've told you that so many times and I... I can't do anything more than try to be there for you."

"Maybe we should go somewhere and be alone," Millie suggests. "We need some time to process everything."

"That sounds good," Darren agrees.

"The jet's been booked," she says suddenly. "I just did. If you weren't coming with me, I would have taken Joy to Hawaii."

Millie grins, and only now do I realize that Joy is standing behind her. She smiles at her friend, but she also looks very upset. I'm sure Millie has confided in her.

"Let's pack," Darren says, pulling her behind him.

They disappear into the house and I look at Joy. She takes a deep breath, crosses her arms in front of her and walks over to me.

"Hi," she says and sits down across from me on the couch where Darren sat a few minutes ago. "So you know too?"

"Darren just blurted it out."

"Yeah," she confirms. "Millie too ... she ... she was crying so much. I didn't know what to do. It probably would have been better if Phoenix or Sienna had been with her." She shrugs.

Does she really think she wasn't the right person to have this conversation with? To be honest, I think Joy was the only one Millie could talk to about it.

"Do you really think that little of yourself as a friend?" I look at her and she shrugs. "Why?"

"Phoe and I have been drifting apart ever since she got pregnant. I'm not good with emotional stuff."

"Joy," I say. "I think you were the only one she could confide in."

"You think so?" Surprise is written all over her face as I laugh softly.

"Sienna is pregnant and certainly the last person Millie could talk to about it. Phoenix already has a child and wouldn't understand either. Understand isn't the right word ... she ... she'll never be able to relate. But you are neither. Even if you can have children, you're not currently in a situation that Millie will never experience."

"It was such a shock to me," she blurts out, looking at me across the table. "She ... she just cried for ages, and I ... I thought it was still about Sadie. Really ... I ... I wanted to tell her to pull herself together. But then ... then this information came out."

"I was shocked too."

"I'm so sorry for Millie," Joy whispers. "She would have been a great mother."

"They have options." I try to reassure Joy. "Adoption or surrogacy, and there is no shortage of money for either."

"There is a difference between carrying the child under your heart for nine months and having it carried by another woman." She looks at me and frowns. "Did I just say that? How sappy."

I laugh and get up to go to her. At first, I expect her to reject me, but Joy just slides over to make room for me.

"You don't always have to be cool and distant," I say, searching her eyes. "Sometimes you're allowed to say sappy things like that. Of course, it's different for a woman to carry a child herself."

"If you say so." Joy grins at me. "Tyler, I... I mean... it... it's none of my business, but... did you sleep with Sophie?"

Surprised that she would bring up the subject right after we talked about Millie's infertility, I pull away. Joy notices and keeps her distance as well.

"I wouldn't call it sleeping."

"Tyler!" Her voice gets louder - shriller. "Yes or no?"

"Yes," I answer honestly and could swear that I heard something like a sob escape her throat. I've known Joy long enough to know she's too restrained for that. "It's not what you think."

"Not what I think?" She laughs. "Can't you come up with a lamer line?"

"Not at the moment," I answer honestly. "What am I supposed to say?"

"I don't know." Joy runs her fingers through her hair and looks at me sideways. Her posture is completely rigid. "You don't owe me anything, but..."

"You don't like it either and you're jealous?" I grin at her and wiggle my eyebrows.

"You're impossible, Tyler Connor." She hits my arm but I catch her hand and pull her to me. Joy falls forward and her free hand lands on my thigh. Our faces are only inches apart and it would be so easy to kiss her. But I'm not stupid and know she doesn't want me to. "Why did you have sex with her?"

17

Joy

Tyler and I drove Millie and Darren to the airport in Melbourne and are now back in the car. Before he could answer my question about sex with Sophie, Millie and Darren were standing in front of us with their bags packed. Darren asked if Tyler would give them a lift and although I would have preferred to talk to him, I didn't say anything. Instead, I offered to go with them so he wouldn't be alone on the way back. I regret that now, as we remain silent. There is no conversation in sight. Tyler doesn't want to answer my question. It's obvious and I can even understand it. I wouldn't tell him if the roles were reversed.

"Fancy a trip to the beach?" His voice breaks the silence in the car and I look over at him.

"Sure," I whisper. "Why not."

I don't care if we go to the beach or not. I don't care if we go anywhere. The main thing is that this oppressive silence has finally ended. Tyler signals and we turn towards the beach.

After a few feet, I see the ocean on the horizon. It glistens in the setting sun and I can't help but smile. Sunsets are a rarity both in Lincoln and back home in Lexington. I find it all the more beautiful now. The last rays of sunlight break through the trees along the road and cast a pleasant light on Tyler. His skin has tanned a lot over the past few days. He looks insanely hot sitting behind the wheel. His right hand grips the steering wheel while his arm rests on the driver's door. His left arm rests on the center console.

"What are you thinking about?" he asks, suddenly breaking the silence, and I bite my lip as if he's caught me doing something forbidden.

"Nothing." Certainly not the most eloquent response. Tyler grins and takes my hand. Without saying anything or showing any emotion, he intertwines our fingers and places our hands on the center console. I say nothing, ignoring the pounding of my heart in my chest. I also try to ignore the fact that he has started to draw little circles on the back of my hand and that he looks so damn sexy behind the wheel of the SUV that I want to sigh with pleasure.

"Nothing?" he asks, looking over at me for a second. "Want to know what I'm thinking?"

"No."

"Afraid of my answer?" He seems relaxed and not at all tense as he says it. Doesn't the whole situation make him nervous?

Of course not. He had the courage to take my hand in his and ask me what I was thinking. Tyler is as cool as a cucumber.

"Then tell me what you're thinking," I answer bitchily, and he laughs softly. I'm glad he's amused.

"I'm thinking about you," he confesses and my head turns. "And don't look at me like Bambi when his mother died. What did you think I was thinking about?"

"I don't know," I answer honestly.

"I was mad at you ... mad at myself ... mad at everything." He sighs. "Then there was Sophie. I approached her ... and ... and we spoke briefly while you were dancing with Kyle all evening."

"So now it's my fault that you couldn't keep your dick in your pants."

"No," he replies. "I never said that. I spoke to her a little bit and got the impression that she was into Kyle. She also asked who you were. Then she wanted to leave."

I look out the passenger window, not daring to look at him. Why did I ask such a stupid question? I don't want to hear him talk about sex with another woman. Just hours before we had sex.

"She asked me if I wanted to go with her, and yes - there was no reason for me not to." I take a deep breath and close my eyes. He only had sex with her. "Do you really want to hear this?"

"Yes," I reply. "Go on."

"We didn't get twenty feet. Somewhere between the bar and a supermarket, in an alley, I fucked her."

"Yuck." That's low, even by my standards. God knows I'm no angel who needs a bed under her, but a back alley is out of the question.

"That's one way to put it," he sighs, steering the SUV into a parking spot. Through the windshield there is a breathtaking view of the Indian Ocean. The sun has almost disappeared behind the horizon. "It was over pretty quick, and then I left."

"Hmm."

"And apparently she's one of those women who doesn't get the one in a one-night stand."

I bite my bottom lip to stop myself from laughing, but I can't. I can't suppress it, and my malicious glee is boundless.

"That's why she was with you today."

"Yeah," he says, turning off the engine. Tyler unbuckles his seat belt and I do the same. I grab my small purse from the floor and get out. After we close the doors, he locks the car and I walk toward him. "And then she clung to me the entire evening. I didn't want to outright reject her. We're guests here."

"So, you'd rather let her figure it out and let me think there's more going on than a quickie in a back alley."

"Apparently." Tyler presses his lips together and stuffs the car keys and his iPhone into his jeans. "Let's head for the water."

Once again, we remain silent until we reach the beach and take off our shoes to walk the last few feet to the water. The waves are gentle and the sun is only a memory.

"Shall we sit down?" Tyler points to the sand. "I mean, only if... if you don't mind. Because of all the sand... you... you know."

"As if sand has ever been a problem for me," I chuckle and sit down. Tyler does the same, settling on the sand next to me.

We look out to sea for a moment before he speaks again.

"I think I've always liked that about you," Tyler says without looking at me. "That uncomplicated toughness. You've never been a typical girl... well... on the inside."

He gives me a grin and looks suggestively at me as he evaluates my body, and I roll my eyes.

"You jumped into the mud puddle instead of tiptoeing around it, you caught the spider and didn't scream for me to get rid of it," he lists my other absolutely feminine qualities. "You never dolled yourself up unnecessarily or wore a hundred pounds of makeup on your face. Of course, you wear more make-up now, but it suits you. You are unconventional and yourself - always."

"Wow." I'm stunned by his speech. I had never seen or

thought of myself that way. "To be honest, none of that makes me sound like a guy magnet."

"Why?" he asks, looking at me. His blue eyes scrutinize me and a smile creeps across his lips. "Because you're not blonde or because you're incredibly shy?"

I nod.

"Joy," he whispers, leaning into me. My heart starts to beat faster and goosebumps spread all over my body as Tyler dances his fingertips along my cheek, finally wrapping a strand of my hair around his finger. "You're perfect for me. Just the way you are."

"Tyler, I..." I'm at a loss for words at this confession.

"Yes, I want to kiss you too."

That's not what I wanted to say, but before I can react, his mouth is on mine. His lips meet mine incredibly softly. He lets my hair fall and puts his hand on the back of my neck instead. I kiss him back and open my mouth slightly for him. Tyler's tongue enters my mouth. He kisses me demandingly, but not too greedily. It's just the right amount of passion and tenderness I need. Boldly, I lean into him, giving him everything I can and feel for him.

I love him.

For over six years.

This kiss makes me feel like it's not too late, that he still believes in us despite all my rejections and excuses.

"Ty," I sigh as we pull away to catch our breath. "I just wanted to say that I..."

"Later," he mumbles, pulling me astride his lap.

My pelvis is pressed against his, and when I wrap my hands around his neck, we both groan. The kiss has clearly sparked something naughty, and we're doing our best to excel at it. Holy shit, he's such a good kisser. I grind against him, pressing my center against his cock as it hardens inside his jeans.

Tyler lets go of my neck and puts his hands on my ass. He starts massaging my butt cheeks and sliding me up and down on his cock.

When his hands go to work on the button of my jeans, I pull away from him, breathing heavily. His lips are slightly parted and the lust in his eyes only makes me hotter, but I can't have sex with him now. At least not without saying something.

"I was an idiot," I begin my apology. "Yeah, I've been looking for as many excuses as possible not to get involved with you. I'm scared, Tyler. Damn scared of the future. I need to know what's going to happen, I need to be in control of it, and a life with you... I won't have that by your side."

"I understand," he says, letting go of my waistband. Tyler puts his hands on my hips and pushes my shirt up as his hands slide underneath. His touch gives me goosebumps again and my skin tingles. "Am I still worth the risk?"

He asks me, without starting a new discussion or explaining the benefits.

"I think so," I admit with a smile. "Seeing you with Sophie ... it ... it broke my heart, Ty. I ... I was so sad and ... and angry and ... yeah."

"Jealous?" As if to help me out, he grins at me. "I think that's the word you're looking for. I've been watching you, babe. You were about to explode and punch her in the face. Not very ladylike either, but hot as hell."

"Tyler." I punch him in the chest and he laughs. Then he leans in again and steals a kiss.

"Say yes to me," he whispers, running his lips from my mouth to my neck. "To a life by my side."

"You're not playing fair." He just laughs when I try to pull away and shamelessly slides his right hand down my jeans and further into my panties until he reaches my mound. "Stop it."

"Oh no, baby," he whispers to me. "We're going to have

amazing sex by the ocean. Then we'll get undressed, have sex in the ocean again, and then in the car...maybe from behind on the hood. I want to have so much kinky sex with you that I won't miss you in the months we'll be apart, or at least enough that I won't need my hand every day."

"Which..." I throw my head back as he slides his middle finger between my labia and penetrates me. "Oh God, Tyler! What... what separation?"

"We'll wait for the draft," he growls as I moan again. "Slip your hand into my pants."

I unzip his jeans with shaky fingers and slide my hand inside and further into his boxers before cupping his hard-on in my hands. The skin is velvety soft and it is hot. I start pumping him with steady strokes as he slides two fingers into my pussy. I moan again and lift my pelvis a little to give him better access.

"We'll wait for the draft," he repeats and I nod. "And if I have to go to New York, you'll still go to Los Angeles."

"Tyler, I..."

"No, Joy," he stops me immediately and looks at me sternly. "You want to work as a psychologist in Los Angeles and I want you to do that. I don't want you in New York just to be with me. It's not right. What do we care what anybody else does or what any reporters or fans think is right? I'd rather have you happy on the other side of the country than in New York with me if you don't want to be there. Maybe new opportunities will open up at some point."

"You ... you're serious?"

"Of course I'm serious." He seems almost offended. "We'll do it our way."

"Yes," I answer and kiss him again. Tyler kisses me back and the thrusts of his fingers speed up.

"Take your pants off. I want all of you."

"Now I have something against sand," I reply and he rolls

his eyes and tears at the fabric of my jeans. "Yes, I do," I exclaim and stand up, pulling my pants and panties down far enough for him to see me naked. Tyler's hand moves between my legs again and the moisture leaking from me wets his fingers. Fuck, that is so hot. He grins at me with satisfaction and rubs it all over his cock.

"Can you get to my wallet?" he wants to know, his voice dripping with lust. "There's a condom in there."

He turns to his left so I can get it out of his back pocket. I quickly open it, pull out the condom and rip open the wrapper. Then I slip the rubber over his hard cock and throw the wallet on the sand next to us.

Tyler pulls me to him by my thighs and positions me over his cock.

"Are you ready?"

"When am I not?" I reply, winking at him.

"Oh God," he moans as I lower my pelvis. "You're still my undoing."

"I hope so," I reply, placing my lips on his.

18

Joy

"Good morning beautiful lady." I giggle and moan the next moment as Tyler pushes himself between my legs. He's not going to... Oh God, he's already inside me. Didn't we go at it all night after we got back to our cabin? "I want to wake you up like this every morning," he says,

"You goofball." I laugh, but still have my eyes closed and enjoy the stretching feeling of his penis inside me. "But yes ... I could get used to it."

He laughs too and wraps my left leg around his hip so he can penetrate me deeper. His pace is slow and easy, but I like it. Yesterday afternoon and evening were anything but slow. After I rode him on the beach, on the sand, we undressed and took a dip in the sea. We held each other in the water but didn't have sex. But it was a different story when we got to the car. Tyler was true to his word when he said he wanted to take me from behind over the hood of the SUV. Or rather on the hood of the SUV, because he's taller than me. Back at the cabin we headed for the shower and went at it again until he licked me into dreamland.

"You're so perfect," he whispers to me, caressing my neck with his lips. "Your pussy is made for me. Damn, baby, you're so hot."

"Hmm," I sigh at his gentle thrusts and push my pelvis towards him. "Take me harder, Tyler."

"No," he whispers against my lips, moving back and forth with lazy thrusts. I dig my fingers into his neck, groaning with every rub of his body against mine. This sex is far too soulful, far too tender to compare to the sex we've had over the past few years and what we did on the beach last night.

"Oh, Tyler," I cry out, my body arching underneath him. He picks up the pace of his thrusts until he comes inside of me.

His body slumps onto mine and Tyler pulls out of me, dropping onto the mattress next to me. I look up at the ceiling and lie still as the mattress sinks next to me. Tyler must have rolled over.

I turn my head to see his satisfied face. There's a broad smile on his lips as he brushes my hair back. "Morning, baby," he repeats, wishing me a good start to the day. "How did you sleep?"

Tyler's fingertips run down my right arm to my hand and on to my stomach.

"Great, and you?" I turn to look into his eyes.

"Me too," he says with a smile and leans in. His lips meet mine and we kiss slowly. We have all the time in the world, and we should make the most of our remaining days on vacation before everyday life in Lincoln demands us back.

"I love your blue hair." My heart leaps at this confession and my stomach starts to tingle. Tyler smiles. "Surprised?"

"All the other women I've seen you with have been blondes."

"Not that subject again." He moans and kisses my lips and then my neck. "Honestly, Jolene... I don't want to hear it again."

"Now I'm Jolene again?" I raise my eyebrows and look at him.

Tyler laughs, his voice rough from sleep.

"You'll always be Jolene to me." He smiles even wider. "Whether you like it or not."

"To be honest," I hesitate before continuing, feeling unexpectedly shy at this moment, "I don't mind... but don't go spreading it around. I've got a reputation to uphold."

"A reputation?" Tyler bursts out laughing. It's funny how relaxed we are with each other. Especially in bed. Naked. After making love all night. "And what exactly is your reputation?"

"Probably not very good." I shrug, trying to make light of it. I know my reputation in college is more along the lines of cheap and easy. But hey, I was just having fun and enjoying my fair share of... sex. No one can hold that against me.

Tyler doesn't answer me, confirming my suspicion.

"Go ahead, ask," I sigh. "It's on the tip of your tongue."

His eyes pierce me and I can tell he wants to know which players on the football team I had sex with. The answer is easier than Tyler suspects. Just Ethan. We had a thing for a few weeks, a year and a half ago. I rarely had sex at the college, preferring to hang out with guys from Lincoln and the surrounding area.

"It's none of my business." Though he tries to make it sound as believable as possible, he turns away and lies on his back. Tyler slides his right arm under his head and wraps his left around me. He pulls me closer and I rest my head on his chest. I draw small circles on his chest with my fingertips. "That was before me - before us."

"I only had sex with Ethan," I say softly. Tyler takes a deep

171

breath and pauses for a few seconds. "But it wasn't serious. We had a brief fling and then you showed up in Lincoln."

As if a balloon was popped with a needle, he exhales, and his chest deflates.

"I mostly dated guys from Lincoln and the surrounding area," I continue. "Never anything serious."

"Until now?" Tyler sounds unsure and his body tenses. Grinning, I lift my head and look at him.

"Until now," I confirm his assumption and press my lips to his.

★★★

It's a miracle that Tyler and I made it out of bed, showered, dressed, and even had a late breakfast by the time Sienna, Denver, Phoenix, and Jake arrive at our cabin in the early afternoon with Charlotte in their arms. I'm sitting on the porch and Tyler is in the house. He wanted to talk to his parents and his new manager. It's about the draft, which still concerns me. If Tyler has to go to New York and I have to live my dream in Los Angeles, I don't know if the distance is going to be too much. We would only see each other every other week, which would be twice a month. Not very appealing, but I don't want to give up my dream. No matter how selfish it may sound to other people. It's an unwritten rule among professional athletes that their personal lives are determined by their club. But I dread the thought of being separated from Tyler.

"Hey!"

"Hey," I answer with a smile and stand up to greet my friends. Sienna and Phoenix look perfect as usual. Their blonde hair falls in soft waves over their shoulders, their makeup is subtle, and they're both wearing floral dresses that make them look more demure than they are. I, on the other hand, have my hair up in a messy bun, barely any makeup by my standards, and am wearing denim shorts and a loose jersey top. Jake and Denver are also in denim shorts and black t-shirts. Baby Charlotte has been dressed by her mother in a pink dress with a matching headband on her head.

"Is Tyler in the house?" Denver asks with a smile after greeting me and I nod.

"Yes," I say. "He's on the phone with his parents, but I think he's done."

"Okay," he says with a grin. "Oh and Joy?"

"Huh?" I look up at him and Denver's grin widens.

I have this nagging feeling that something's not right. Jake can't contain his laughter anymore, and Phoenix and Sienna are trying to keep straight faces. But even they are pressing their lips together to stifle laughter.

"Nice hickey." Denver taps his neck with his index finger and winks at me. "Did Tyler finally give it to you?"

My jaw drops and my right hand lands on my neck with a loud smack that only makes Denver and Jake laugh harder.

"You, in the house," Phoenix cries, pushing her brother away. "You guys are impossible, and besides, I was going to drop the bomb. You've ruined it for me."

She can't be serious? Is that why she's mad at him? I roll my eyes. I probably wouldn't have been able to keep it to myself if the tables were turned. I reach for my iPhone, which is on the coffee table in front of me, and turn on the front camera.

"Holy shit," I gasp, frantically rubbing the bruise on my neck. "I'm going to kill him."

Denver and Jake are still laughing when they finally disappear into the house, and I throw my iPhone back on the table in front of me. Then I flop down on the wicker couch and look at my friends. Sienna and Phoenix are bursting with curiosity.

"Go ahead, ask away."

"When, how, where and ..." Phoenix laughs devilishly. "How many times?"

"Phoe." Sienna tries to act outraged but can't help grinning. "You can be a little more subtle."

"No way," Phoenix replies. "She would never be subtle."

I roll my eyes. Sienna seems to think about it, then nods.

"That's true," she says, amused, looking at me intently. "Answer her questions, Joy."

I sigh but have to smile anyway. The thought of last night and this morning warms my heart and the butterflies in my stomach pick up speed again.

"What can I say?" I squirm. Somehow, it's hard for me to talk about sex right now. Me, of all people, who never minces words when it comes to the most beautiful thing in the world, I'm embarrassed. Unbelievable.

"At least something more than that goofy look would be nice," Phoenix says dryly, gesturing in my direction, urging me to start talking.

"We drove Millie and Darren to the airport in Melbourne," I say, looking back and forth between my friends. "You know about that?"

They both nod.

"Before Darren asked Tyler if he would drive them, we had already started to reconcile."

"You were making out?"

"We were talking, Phoe." I roll my eyes. "On the way back from the airport, Tyler asked if I wanted to go to the beach. I said yes. Then we talked things out and... and decided to give it a shot. We want to give it a try, on the understanding that he does his thing and I do mine."

Sienna and Phoenix are silent for a moment, looking at each other, until Phoenix finally sighs and turns back to me.

"And you think that will work?"

174

"I don't know," I say honestly. "That's where things stand right now. I know Tyler wouldn't say no if I wanted to go with him. We want to wait for the draft."

"Okay," Sienna says. "What happened next? Did you have sex? On the beach?"

I can't help but grin broadly. Once again, the images of me riding him in the sand and us doing it later on in the car come to mind.

"You had sex on the beach," Sienna exclaims, digging her fingers into my arm. "How was it?"

"Good," I answer, and when I realize she's not satisfied with the answer, I groan. "It was damn good. Perfect. Okay? We didn't have sex in the ocean, but afterwards on the hood and..."

"Wait." Phoenix holds up her hand to stop me. "On the hood?" She points to the black SUV parked in front of the house and I nod.

"Well," I stammer. "Maybe Tyler bent me over and took me from behind."

"Oh my God," my friends squeal.

"That's really hot," Sienna adds, and from the dreamy look on her face, I don't want to know what she's thinking. God, I really don't. Because this experience belongs to Tyler and me.

"And you're together now?" Phoenix asks, steering the conversation back into much safer territory.

"Yes." I smile lovingly. "We want to try."

"We're so happy for you." They jump up and pounce on me. "Joy is in love and has a boyfriend." They are more excited than I am.

They release me and sit down. Phoenix next to me and Sienna in the chair across from me. Suddenly they get very serious.

"Millie," Sienna says quietly. "She called us and told us on the phone. She said that you... she... Tyler and you know. That we should please tell Jake and Denver. Darren didn't want to discuss it."

"Yeah." I clear my throat. "After it came out that Tyler had sex with Sophie... she... followed me. I was able to get over it pretty quickly, but she started crying again and... and I wanted to ask her if she was being paranoid. I mean, I... I'm not really Darren's friend, but I know he loves her."

Phoenix and Sienna nod in agreement. Both are quiet and introspective. Sienna's hands are on her stomach. The thought of not being able to have a baby must be horrible for her.

"Then she blurted it out," I continue. "I tried to calm her down and we talked for a long time. Then Millie decided to fly back home with Darren and work it out together."

"And I'm pregnant and talk about it all the time." Sienna shakes her head, placing her hands on her cheeks. "I feel so bad for Millie."

"She didn't say it, but I suspect she didn't want to spoil your excitement about the baby." I have no idea if that's the case, but it seems obvious to me. "And not to spoil your happiness with Charlotte."

"Millie would make a great mother," Phoenix says with a smile. I smile back and so does Sienna.

The door opens and Tyler, Denver and Jake with Charlotte come out and join us. The little girl immediately reaches for her mother. Phoenix places her daughter on her lap and I stand up to let Jake sit next to her. "Thanks," he says and I take the empty chair next to him.

Tyler sits down next to me on the arm of my chair and puts his hand on my neck. I flinch at first because I'm not used to such physical closeness. But he doesn't say anything as he begins to massage my neck.

"Have you discussed Millie and Darren?" Denver is the

first to speak, wrapping his arms tighter around Sienna and the baby in her belly. It's an awful feeling for all of us that our best friends are in so much pain.

"Yes," I say, automatically moving closer to Tyler. "Did you?"

"Yeah," he replies. "Darren's not answering us."

"Millie said he doesn't want to talk about it," Phoenix says. "We should give them the time they need."

We all nod and Tyler puts his arm around my shoulders to pull me closer.

"Okay," Jake says, clapping his hands to break the tension. "Let's go into town and get some burgers. I'll pay."

Relieved, we get up and head for the cars.

"What do you say we take another trip to the ocean later?" Tyler asks, pulling me close. He puts his arms around me and gently presses his lips to mine. I kiss him back and snuggle against him. My hands rest on the nape of his neck and I stroke his skin with my fingertips.

"Sounds good," I agree. "Same program as yesterday?"

He just laughs and kisses me again.

19

Joy

Las Vegas, one and a half months later

Almost two months have passed since our vacation in Australia. A time in which Tyler and I got to know each other even better and realized that we belong together. Even the draft and a possible team selection on the other side of the country won't keep us apart. After we returned to Lincoln, his entire focus was on this weekend. Tyler would never admit it, but it makes him nervous as hell. After all, it will define his entire life for the next few years, and mine as well. I started writing my thesis and haven't had much time to think about the draft. But we've been in Las Vegas for two days now and the mega-event in the desert is getting closer and closer. All of Las Vegas is getting ready for this year's draft. It's a huge adventure for us and I'm very happy to be sharing it with my three best friends and the love of my life. Jake, Denver and Darren are also here.

Things are going really well between Millie and Darren. They've talked a lot about their problem with conception.

They don't want a child right now anyway, and when the time comes, they have all the financial resources to make it happen through adoption or surrogacy. Millie also spoke a lot to Sienna, who is her best friend. She never wanted Sienna to feel like she wasn't happy she was pregnant. But she also said that she needed some space first.

Sienna is now well into her twentieth week of pregnancy and she has a cute little baby bump developing. We don't know the sex yet. They are keeping it a secret. Phoenix is sure it's a boy, even though she was betting on a girl. She thinks that Sienna's belly has a different shape to how hers looked when she was pregnant with Charlotte.

Hand in hand, Tyler and I follow Millie and Darren into the huge hall where the draft is being held. The logo of this year's draft and the main sponsors are alternately displayed on three adjacent video screens.

In front of them are at least ten rows of chairs for the fans of the various clubs, who have been allowed to enter the hall behind us. Tyler gently squeezes my hand and smiles at me. He's been on edge for days, but today he's even worse. The nervousness is eating away at him. All the experts, Coach Flanders, his dad and Millie, have predicted that he's going to be a first-round pick. That would be good for us because then we can enjoy the next two days. Darren, Jake and Denver also have a good chance of being drafted today. Lincoln College is very well represented this year.

The security guards flank us on both sides, and one of them, who has been assigned to the boys, talks excitedly to Darren until Millie gives her a look to be quiet. Her grandfather is about to announce the first draft pick for the Minneapolis Warriors.

"That's where we're sitting." Millie turns to Tyler and me and points to a cozy booth in the corner.

Behind us are Tyler's parents, Monica and Kurt, and Darren's sister, Dana, who, to his surprise, has come all the way from Texas. His parents still show no interest in his passion for sports and unlike the parents of the other guys, don't support him at all.

Denver and Phoenix's parents Mrs. Jones, her partner John, along with their youngest sister Madison and her boyfriend Fynn as well as Jake's parents are also present. This completes the Jones-Sullivan family. It's hard to believe that Tyler, Jake and I are only children. Millie's sister Maya sits with her grandfather. Millie passed up playing a leading role in the McDonald dynasty today to be with Darren.

"This is incredible," I marvel, pulling my iPhone out of my clutch to snap a picture.

"Totally." Tyler's mom smiles kindly at me.

When his parents found out we were a couple, his mom wanted to pack up and move to Lincoln. Luckily, Tyler was able to convince her that it wasn't such a good idea. My parents were very excited as well. I could literally feel the weight of several tons lift from my mother's heart because I had finally found a man. I didn't fulfill her wish that my rebellious phase, as she calls my blue hair - now pink - and my elaborate makeup, is over.

Two weeks ago, the ends of my hair which had been blue for almost two years turned pink. Tyler looked at me skeptically at first. I knew how much he liked my blue ends, but then he was thrilled. Today I'm wearing a black jumpsuit with wide straps that go straight over my shoulders and create a dizzyingly deep neckline. My breasts are held in place by an adhesive bra. Needless to say, Tyler's eyes remained glued to them for minutes after I emerged from the bathroom. I added subtle jewelry and smoky eyes. My hair is loose and twisted into big beach waves.

I look at my boyfriend and grin. Tyler looks gorgeous and I want to drag him into the nearest broom closet and have sex with him. Although we do it all the time anyway - to keep him in shape. The black suit with the crisp white shirt looks incredible on him. His hair is casually styled with gel. His well groomed three-day beard completes the picture.

Millie and I sit next to each other between Tyler and Darren so that the executive assistant and other interviewees can sit next to them if necessary.

"I have to tell you again how hot you look." I nod approvingly at Millie.

She's wearing the famous dress, as Darren calls it, that she wore to the dinner at Dana's aborted wedding. It's red, has a deep plunging neckline, and is held up at the neck by two thin gold chains. The slit in the leg goes all the way up to her hip. Darren says the dress brings them luck. Her blood-red lips and blonde hair tied loosely at the back of her head make her irresistible tonight.

"You too," she replies with a grin and winks at me.

I turn to Tyler and place my hand on his. He clasps it gently and looks at me. "What do you think?" he whispers.

"That this is all pretty unbelievable, and you?"

"Me too." He laughs softly and blows a kiss just below my earlobe, giving me goosebumps. "You're the most beautiful woman here tonight."

"You think so?"

"Baby," he moans and kisses me hard. "You can just thank me for the compliment."

"Thank you," I giggle and kiss him again.

For the next hour, Tyler spends his time making conversation and introducing me as his partner. I get excited every time and smile at all the important club representatives. Tyler, on the other hand, seems very relaxed as he talks to them and shakes their hands.

"Grandpa!" Millie jumps up and hugs her grandfather. "What are you doing here?"

"I could say I came to see my little girl, but I'd be lying." He winks at her and greets Darren with a hug. He extends his hand to Tyler and me. "Are you guys nervous?"

"Totally," they assure him in unison.

"I've got my eye on you."

"Grandpa," Millie squeals, probably trying to cover his mouth. "You promised me you wouldn't say anything."

"Sorry, honey." He kisses her cheek and nods to the three of us again.

"Now I'm nervous," Millie pouts and Darren pulls her close and whispers something to her. When her face turns as red as her dress, I'm sure it was something naughty.

"I know what he said," Tyler whispers to me and I laugh.

"What?" I raise my eyebrows and look at him eagerly.

"I've known Darren long enough to know that he told her he wanted to have sex with her."

"I said I loved her," Darren interjects. "Not everyone is horny all the time."

"Except you," Tyler counters, pulling me closer. "I want you too - you know."

"Of course," I laugh, and before he can say anything else, the executive assistant taps him on the shoulder.

"Mr. Connor," she says, "this is Mr. Brooks. He's the General Manager of the Los Angeles Tigers."

Mr. Brooks is an extremely attractive man, in his fifties, I would guess. He's a little shorter than Tyler, but still very fit. His broad shoulders and chest fill out the tailored suit perfectly. His graying hair is slicked back with gel.

At the mention of my dream city, I immediately tense up. It's a good sign when the CEO comes to see you in person, right? But I shouldn't get my hopes up too high. The Tigers are doing well in the league and are in the middle of the draft. I did my homework to narrow down the teams that might have real interest in Tyler. Millie, however, ruined all my research in a matter of seconds. True to the motto: Anything can happen in the draft!

"Of course," Tyler says graciously, shaking Mr. Brooks' hand. "It's a pleasure to meet you."

"The pleasure is all mine," he replies, looking at me. "And who is your lovely companion?" Tyler wraps his arm tighter around me and pulls me close.

"My girlfriend Jolene," he introduces me with a smile.

"Hello," I reply friendly and shake Mr. Brook's hand. His handshake is firm and thankfully not sweaty. I've experienced a few of those today.

"Nice to meet you, Jolene," he says and I nod. By now I've gotten used to my name again. That's probably because neither Tyler nor my parents call me Joy.

"You too." But he hardly hears my reply. He has already turned to Millie.

"Millie," he says.

"Uncle Jeff," my friend greets him, giving him a big hug. "This is Darren." Tyler groans and we sit back down and I lean toward him.

"Everything okay?" I ask and he nods.

"Sure," he says and reaches for a bottle of water that is in a basket on the table in front of us.

"Sure?" I can tell there is something bothering him. He was in a much better mood before the conversation with Mr. Brooks, who is now praising Darren to the rafters. I knew there was going to be some tension between the guys at some point, because Darren has been the favorite and invited to tryouts by every scout - literally every one of them - in the last few weeks and months. Even teams that have absolutely no need for his position. The reason is obvious - Millie! Nobody wants to mess with a McDonald. Sienna, Phoenix and I have tried to explain to our friends that it's not always better to be seen by everyone. But that was of little consolation to them.

"Hey," I whisper. "You're really good."

"Thanks, baby." Tyler sighs and kisses me as the noise around us grows louder.

The event has begun.

★★★

Tyler's tension almost physically pains me. He can't relax for a second, and with every pick that passes where he isn't selected, his shoulders slump further. It hurts me to see him like this and not be able to do anything about it. Denver and Jake, sitting a few seats away from us, haven't been drafted yet either.

"Next up, the Austin Guns will announce their pick." The announcer's voice booms through the speakers. "Please welcome Timothy Gardens, quarterback for the Austin Guns from 1990 to 1999."

Applause roars through the room, and I clap too, until the former player raises his hands and laughingly asks the crowd to stop applauding. "Good evening, Las Vegas," he greets us. "It's a great honor for me to announce the first-round pick for your Austin Guns and mine in this year's NFL Draft."

Another round of applause and I reach for Tyler's hand and squeeze it. He looks over at me and smiles.

"The Austin Guns pick in this year's NFL Draft..." I hold my breath as he pauses for dramatic effect. My body is tense and I squeeze Tyler's hand harder than necessary. This event is turning me into a nervous wreck. "Denver Jones - Quarterback

- Lincoln College."

We jump to our feet. All four of us. Millie, Darren, Tyler and me. And we clap for Denver.

He can't believe it himself and holds his hands over his face while Sienna hugs him. Jake and Phoenix approach him as well.

"Denver," Tyler and Darren cheer. They both pump their fists in the air. "You did it."

Denver stands and hugs Sienna first. He kisses her and then hugs his sisters and mother. Finally, Jake, John, Fynn and other well-wishers lining his path to the stage. We continue to clap.

"He did it," Tyler says next to me, and I know these words come from the bottom of his heart. The four of them are ecstatic for each other because they are true friends and they know how hard they have worked over the last few years for this weekend.

Denver steps onto the stage and accepts the congratulations and the Austin Guns jersey. He also receives a baseball cap with the Austin Guns logo, a firing cannon.

"Wow." Overwhelmed, he wipes away tears. Thank you to everyone who made today possible...that's what the guys who got to stand here before me said." Denver takes a breath. "I want to thank the Austin Guns for having the faith in me to select me today. Then I want to thank my friends who have always supported me, my mom and my sisters. To my dad, who ... who should have been here today ..." Denver sobs and I look at Sienna who, like Denver's sisters and mom, are fighting back tears. I reach for Tyler's hand and squeeze it. "And I... I want to thank my wonder girlfriend who will be accompanying me on this journey and reminding me that I'm not alone down there in the hot south. And Darren? I look forward to seeing you in your city."

Denver leaves the stage and returns to Sienna and his family.

Next up is the Carolina Lions pick. They have a former linebacker introducing the first-round pick.

"The Carolina Lions pick for this year's NFL Draft..." He makes the same annoying pause. "Jake Sullivan - Running Back - Lincoln College."

Again, we jump up and clap for Jake, giving him as much credit as Denver. He hugs Phoenix first, kisses her, and whispers something to her.

"They're moving to Charlotte with Charlotte," Millie calls to me laughing, "you can't make this stuff up."

I laugh too and Tyler puts his arms around me. Jake steps onto the stage, just like Denver before him. "Wow," he begins his speech. "I want to thank the Carolina Lions, my family and, of course, the most incredible woman by my side - Phoenix. I can't wait to start our new life with Charlotte in Charlotte."

Accompanied by applause, Jake leaves the stage and returns to Phoenix and his parents.

Countless more picks go by without either Darren or Tyler being chosen. We're already in the third round. The guys get more and more nervous as Millie's grandfather takes the stage.

"Good evening," he says. "It's a great honor to announce the selection for the Minneapolis Warriors."

Millie tenses up, sitting as straight as she can. Darren sits up as well. Her grandpa isn't going to draft Darren, is he? I can't believe it. That would be a nightmare for both of them, even if they'd never admit it. Millie definitely doesn't want Darren to be her player one day, and I can understand that.

"The Minneapolis Warriors selection in this year's NFL Draft..." he announces. "Tyler Connor - Running Back - Lincoln College. Come join my team, young man."

The room goes wild. Millie and Darren stare at us. I feel

like I can't breathe because I can't believe it. Tyler has found a team - Millie's team! He's going to be a Warrior and we're moving to *fucking* Minnesota.

We? Did I just think we? Fuck yeah!

I love him and there's no way I'm letting him go there alone.

Tyler, like Denver before him, cracks and doesn't move until I touch him.

"Baby," I address him. "Honey, you're in the NFL."

He slowly lifts his head, his eyes moist. Just as I'm about to tell him that I'm with him and will go with him, he takes my face in his hands and kisses me passionately. Oh shit, I wasn't expecting that. My heart does a somersault and the blood rushes through my veins. There's so much adrenaline racing through my body.

"I did it," are the first words he says to me. "I have a team and ... and what a team. Babe, I got a team."

"I know," I sob, and Tyler wipes away my tears. "I love you and ... and I'm so excited about the future."

I don't realize until it's out that I've told him I love him for the first time.

"I love you too," he admits and kisses me one last time. Then he finally gets up and walks to the stage. My heartbeat refuses to slow down, and when I feel Millie's hug, I'm able to let go of a little tension for the first time.

"Congratulations," she says, "welcome to my team."

"Thanks," I giggle, wiping away my tears again. "I can't wait."

"You're actually coming with him?" she asks, her eyes wide.

I know I've been vehemently saying I'm going to Los Angeles for the past few weeks, but I can't. I love Tyler and I want to be by his side.

"I guess." I laugh, hoping that my flood of tears will finally stop.

Tyler steps up to the microphone and, like all the other players, thanks his new team for their trust.

"Then I'd like to thank my parents, who have always supported me, and my girlfriend. Thank you."

I'm glad he keeps it short and doesn't make an overly emotional speech about our love. That wouldn't suit us.

Tyler meets Millie's grandfather again and gets a hug from him. Then he comes down from the stage and approaches me. I put my arms around him and kiss him. He kisses me back and puts the baseball cap he's been given on my head.

"I hope you have enough winter clothes," he says, furrowing his brow. "I mean... I... forget what I've been saying the last few weeks. I can't do this without you, Jolene. I need you there."

"I know." I give him a sincere smile. "What can Los Angeles offer me when the hottest man in the country is in Minnesota?"

Tyler opens his mouth to say something, but ultimately, words fail him and he pulls me close. Overjoyed, he presses his lips to mine.

When we sit down again, Millie's grandfather is still standing on the stage.

"Why isn't he leaving?" I ask Millie.

"We traded with San Francisco to get another pick. It's his turn again."

"Oh," I murmur. "Okay."

I reach for Tyler's hand and intertwine our fingers. He smiles at me, overjoyed, and I can see how relieved he is. Honestly, I am too. I couldn't bear this tension for another pick.

"The Minneapolis Warriors also selected for this year's NFL Draft," Millie's grandfather reads from the card. "Darren Andrews - Defensive End - Lincoln College."

Epilogue

Joy

Hawaii, Five years later

The narrow road leading to Millie and Darren's property in Hawaii is lined with palm trees on the left and a deep chasm into the Pacific Ocean on the right. Our friends are getting married the day after tomorrow and we've all been invited. Tyler and me, Denver and Sienna, and, of course, Jake and Phoenix.

For the past five years, we've managed to stay friends even though we've lived in different parts of the country. After the draft, I graduated from Lincoln with a bachelor's degree in psychology and moved in with Tyler in Minneapolis that fall. There, I enrolled in the University of Minnesota's master's program in sports psychology and, upon graduation, began working at a clinic for athletes founded by the McDonalds.

Tyler got off to a perfect start with the Minneapolis Warriors, fitting right in with the team. The city in the north of the USA became our home, we are happy there and got married almost three years ago. I still can't believe I was the first in our group to get married. I always thought it would be Millie or Sienna. I was the least likely to be called wife.

Millie is getting married the day after tomorrow and when Sienna and Phoenix will get married is up in the air. They aren't even engaged yet.

Since we got married, I go by Jolene Connor-Lin. I didn't want to give up my last name after we got married because it reminds me of my Asian roots. Another reason for the wedding was the unplanned pregnancy with our twins. We hadn't planned to have children, I had just started my job at the clinic. The positive pregnancy test came as a shock, and almost nine months later our twins, Tyra and Jonah, were born. A girl and a boy, the perfect mix. For me, my family planning was over, but my husband felt he had to prove to me what good swimmers his sperm were. Almost two years after Tyra and Jonah were born, I fell pregnant again. Kyra completes our family. With three small children, I decided to quit my job for the time being. I love being with my kids, even though I never thought I would be the one with the most kids out of the four of us.

Jake and Phoenix only have Charlotte. She is five years old and started preschool this year. They now live back in Chicago where Jake signed with the Chicago Eagles. Denver and Sienna's son Austin was born, as his name suggests, in Austin. Their daughter, Feline, was born three months ago. When they named their daughter Feline, Sienna and Denver broke with the Jones tradition of naming their daughter after a city.

Millie and Darren needed time to come to terms with their fate after Millie's diagnosis five years ago. Millie joined the McDonald's family business sooner than expected and has been managing the Minneapolis Warriors for six months. Tyler says she's a good and fair boss. She and Darren don't have children, but Millie is a very involved aunt. Since Tyler and

I are both only children, we chose our friends to be our children's godparents. Darren is Jonah's godfather and Millie is Kyra's godmother. Phoenix is Tyra's godmother. Millie spoils my kids way too much. Since we live right down the street from her, she sees them a lot more than Phoenix does.

"Mommy." Tyra tugs on my dress and I turn to face her. With three kids, we had to rent a minivan instead of a limo. "Are we there yet?"

"We're almost there," I answer and she rolls her eyes. Tyler, sitting across from me, grins.

"Daddy," Tyra tries again. "When is almost?"

"We just have to go over the next hill," he tells her, and she presses her little hands and nose against the van's window to see the hill.

"Don't butter her up," I say, sticking my tongue out at him behind Tyra's back.

Tyler leans over and gives me a soft kiss.

"I think I have the same effect on our daughters as I do on their mother."

"Dream on," I giggle.

"Mommy, mommy, mommy," Tyra calls eagerly from her car seat. "There's the house."

I lean over to her and can now see the impressive mansion. When Millie bought the house six years ago, it had plenty of green space around it. Since then, she has added a large guesthouse and another smaller bungalow so there would always be room for guests.

"I can see it," I say, brushing Kyra's black hair back and securing it with a pink clip. My daughter is the spitting image of me, and Jonah looks a lot like me, too. During the pregnancy, we weren't sure how much my Asian roots would influence our children. The twins more than Kyra. Tyler even dared to claim at one point that he, too, finally had a child. Needless to say,

I didn't find it funny and wanted to wring his neck. Tyra and Jonah are unmistakably his kids. They both have his boundless patience to wheedle everything they want out of me. In Tyler's case, it eventually led to marriage and three children.

Me, I was always sure I wasn't cut out for this kind of life.

Jonah's head is turned to the side, sleeping peacefully. He is holding the teddy bear Darren gave him when he was born. Of course, the teddy bear is wearing Darren's jersey with his number and Jonah's name on it. Tyler almost killed his best friend at the time. Jonah loves the teddy bear. He takes it everywhere. He's also wearing this insanely cute set from Phoenix's latest collection today.

Yeah, from Phoenix's collection – my best friend is one of the hottest children's fashion designers in the country. After being the problem child of our group for a long time, she studied fashion in Charlotte and specializes in children's clothing. Her brand is called Charlotte's Dream. She is incredibly good and has even been asked to show at New York Fashion Week and has shown her designs in Milan. Her collections are exclusive and usually sell out so fast that we pick out the best pieces for our children in advance. Almost everything in my kids' wardrobes is from Phoenix. Kyra's white and blue striped dress with a pink Hawaiian flower sewn on the left breast is also from Phoenix. Only Kyra's onesie is from a no-name brand. I don't like dressing a baby in designer clothes all the time. Millie regularly despairs about it.

The van pulls up to the mansion and Millie rushes out.

"Aunt Millie," Tyra yells, and I roll my eyes. My daughter can't contain herself when she sees Millie or Darren. Tyler and I have stipulated in our will, even though it's very early that if anything happens to us, our children will live with Millie and Darren. They aren't very close to their grandparents because of the distance to Kentucky. After us, Millie and Darren are

194

their primary caregivers. We discussed this at length with our parents, who finally agreed. I unbuckle Kyra and help her out of her seat. She runs to the door of the van and stands on tip-toe to look out the window.

Then the door opens, and I am grateful that Millie has such good reflexes because just as the staff opens the door, Tyra leaps into her arms. It's horrifying to think that our daughter would have fallen flat on her face on the hard asphalt because once again she can't wait.

Tyler and I unbuckle as well. He removes Jonah from his car seat and gently wakes our son. I lift Kyra out of her Maxi-Cosi.

"Hi, guys," Millie greets us. She's wearing a short floral dress and her hair is in a messy bun.

"Hey," I say, resting Kyra's sleeping head on my shoulder.

"Hi." Darren steps up next to Millie, looking just as disheveled. His hair is tousled, and I could swear the label on Darren's Dolce & Gabbana T-shirt usually sits at the back of his neck, not on his chest.

"Do we want to know what you guys were up to before we arrived?" Tyler asks.

"Love," Darren answers and winks. Millie still blushes after all these years. Love, of course. I suspect they were having wild sex on some shelf in this dream house.

"Uncle Darren." Jonah reaches out to him and he takes him in his arms.

"Hey, buddy," Darren greets his godson, as he always does. "Dana and Scott arrived earlier. Pearl's still sleeping."

Fun fact: Dana has been married to Sadie's brother Scott for a year and they have a daughter named Pearl.

Another fun fact: Sadie is now Millie's sister-in-law.

A few months after our trip to Australia, Dana went to visit the O'Malley's. She went there on Darren's advice to learn about cattle breeding and met Scott. They fell in love, and she moved to Melbourne, where they eventually married and became the parents of little Pearl.

But that's another story.

Tyler gets out of the van before me and takes our daughter from me. The driver has kindly prepared the stroller for Kyra. Tyler puts Kyra in it and helps me out of the vehicle.

"Is there anything else you need, Mr. Connor?" the driver asks politely after I get out, and my husband shakes his head.

"No, thank you," he replies.

Tyler leads me away from the van, where our luggage and the double stroller are still being unloaded. He pulls me to his side and wraps his left arm around my waist.

Grinning, I snuggle up to him and put my hands on the back of his neck. Tyler is wearing a white shirt with thin stripes that match Tyra's dress. He's also wearing beige chinos and black Birkenstocks.

"I can't believe we've been married for three years," he muses.

"I can't believe we've been together for five years, married for three, and have three kids," I add. "It wasn't planned."

"Who needs planning?" He looks at me intently and smiles. "You're the best thing that ever happened to me – you guys are the best thing that ever happened to me."

"That's true," I answer with a smile and kiss him gently.

"And I'm still as crazy about you as I was on the first day," Tyler adds and I roll my eyes. Sometimes I wonder why he proposed to me in a sea of red roses instead of asking, "Up for marriage, babe"?

"Tonight, we're going to sneak down to the beach and make out."

Laughing, I throw my head back and playfully punch him in the chest. Whenever we're on vacation and there's a beach

196

nearby, we have sex there. It's a tradition we've kept since that night in Australia.

"We have three children."

"And they have godparents," he points out, referring to the fact that we're staying at Millie and Darren's mansion. "Come on, don't you want to? How about a fourth child?"

"No way!" I exclaim, pulling away from Tyler and walking towards the house. "We can have fun, but just for the sake of it."

"Why not?" Tyler grumbles in all seriousness and I roll my eyes.

"We talked about this, baby."

"That was before Kyra."

Unfortunately, he's right. Before I got pregnant with Kyra, I told him I was perfectly happy with the twins. Of course, we succeeded in conceiving another child.

"Tyler," I call out. "No."

"All right." He catches up to me and puts his arm around me. "I love you."

"I love you too," I say, kissing him gently.

★★★

Moved, I turn around as the music begins to play and proudly see my twins, as well as Austin and Charlotte, throwing flowers. The girls are wearing pale pink dresses with petticoat skirts. Their hair is in braids and they have flower crowns on their heads. Austin and Jonah are wearing black suits with light blue bow ties. I'd love to take pictures of the whole thing, but there's a photographer for that. Tyler grabs my hand and we intertwine our fingers. Jake and Phoenix sit next to us. Denver and Sienna are in the row in front of us. Kyra and Feline's strollers are in the shade on the left. Two nannies sit next to them to take care of them if anything should happen during the ceremony.

"They're doing better than I thought," my husband whispers to me, and I nod. They really are. When we practiced this at home the last few weeks, Tyra dumped the basket after three steps. Yesterday at the dress rehearsal, however, it worked. I suspect she looks up to Charlotte, who is almost twice her age, and that's helping her. With her long blonde hair, Charlotte is the spitting image of her mother. She has absolutely nothing of Jake in her. According to Phoenix, Austin looks a lot like Denver. Feline will hopefully take after her mother more.

"Yeah, right?" I look at Tyler. He looks great in his dark blue tailored suit with a vest and white shirt.

"Hi, Mommy, hi, Daddy," Tyra calls out, waving to us. Embarrassed, I wave back. At three years old, she doesn't realize she's disrupting Millie's walk down the aisle. But I can understand that she wants us to notice her. Millie smiles and winks at me. Her dad walks her down the aisle.

The kids are doing really well and when they get to where Darren is standing waiting, Millie's dad places her hand in Darren's.

Tyler squeezes my hand and reminds us both of the moment my dad put my hand in his. Even though it's been three years since our wedding, those are the moments we'll never forget.

★★★

With a glass of red wine in hand, Phoenix and I join Millie and Sienna on the patio. The party is in full swing inside, but we're taking a moment to enjoy some peace and quiet with the bride. Millie looks beautiful in her floor-length white gown. It's strapless, with a corsage embroidered with tiny pearls. The skirt is made of a flowing fabric with a slightly puffy under-skirt. Millie chose not to wear a hoop skirt, which is typical for wedding dresses. It's a custom-made dress from Barcelona.

I smile at Millie. She's been radiant all day.

"So, Mrs. Andrews," Phoenix giggles. "How does it feel to be a married woman?"

"Great." Millie smiles. "I can't believe I married him."

"I can't believe you didn't try another dick before you said I do."

Sienna and Phoenix burst out laughing. Yes, even after three kids and a wonderful marriage, I can't keep my mouth shut. Millie rolls her eyes.

"Aren't you the one who's been married for over three years and was the first of us to get married? And three, I repeat, three children. So much for one dick topic." Millie shrugs and sips her champagne. "You've become such a mom, Joy."

"You take that back." I wag my index finger admonishing-ly and look at her indignantly. I haven't become a mom just because I have three kids and I'm married. "Our sex life has never been better. In fact, Tyler wants a fourth child."

"Seriously?" Phoenix asks, looking at me with big eyes.

"Yes." I roll my eyes. "He thinks it would be nice."

"And you don't want another one?" Sienna asks, taking a sip of her champagne.

"No," I say, almost indignant at having to explain this to my friends. "After the twins, I thought I was done. A fourth child is definitely not in the plan. What about you guys?" The question is mainly directed at Phoenix. Now we can talk freely in Millie's presence. She is at peace with herself, the situation and her career.

"We're done at two." Sienna raises her hands. "A girl and a boy. Denver and I agree."

"Phoe?" I ask.

"Charlotte was an accident," she blurts out the truth about her daughter. Yes, Charlotte definitely was. When Phoenix got pregnant at nineteen, we were all more than surprised. "She will be six this year. We are thinking of trying again."

"Thinking about it or already trying?"

"We're trying." Phoenix grins broadly. "But not pressure. I'm off the pill and when it happens, it happens. Jake and I want another child, yes, but we won't be upset if we don't have another one. Although I would like it for Charlotte. I loved growing up with my brother and sister."

"With Denver too?" I ask and Phoenix laughs.

"With Denver too," she giggles as he, Darren, Jake, and Tyler approach us.

All four are wearing dark blue suits. It was important to Darren that his buddies and Tyler as his best man wore the same suits.

"Where's my beautiful wife?" Darren asks and Sienna makes room for him to sit next to her. Darren sits down on the bench and pulls Millie close to him.

Tyler wraps his arms around me and kisses my shoulder. I don't miss his look at my cleavage. He's been in love with my floor-length, plunging green dress ever since I showed it to him two weeks ago.

"What are you talking about?" Denver asks with a smile.

"Kids," Sienna replies, snuggling up to him.

"Kids?" Denver grins. "Is that a request?" To emphasize his words, he pulls Sienna against him and grabs her bottom.

"Not in front of me!" exclaims Phoenix.

Even after all these years, the Jones siblings have not come to terms with each other's love lives.

"It really is a never-ending story with you two," I say.

"Not just that," Tyler interjects, pulling me even closer. "And no pressure, but when does Sienna become a Jones and

Phoenix cease to be Jones?"

Suddenly, Denver and Jake become incredibly thirsty. They're gone. Fortunately, Phoenix and Sienna take it in good humor. Although I'm pretty sure, Sienna is slowly considering taking that step.

I look at Tyler and laugh.

"Not everyone can be as brave as you." I reach for the lapels of his jacket and pull him to me. "The question of questions has to be well thought out."

"Right," Darren interjects with a grin. "Asking you to marry him aged me by years."

"Oh, you poor man." I roll my eyes and wink at Darren. Our relationship has improved tremendously over the past few years. We still tease each other, but we don't fight like we used to. "I'm sure you gave Tyler advice and support," I philosophize. "I'm sure of that."

"Especially with Bourbon," Darren says curtly. "He genuinely wanted to marry you. But he'd already knocked you up by then."

"Darren," Millie calls out. "You're a married man now. Stop it."

"Am I?" He stands and pulls her with him. Phoenix, Sienna, Tyler and I laugh as Darren throws Millie over his shoulder and carries her down to the beach. "Then my wife can be of service to me now. You have duties."

"We should get out of here," Phoenix says and Sienna, Tyler and I nod.

"You're leaving me alone with him?" Millie asks, hanging upside down over Darren's shoulder.

"You married him," Phoenix says with a shrug. "It's too late for that question."

Tyler puts his arm around me and leads me into the house behind Phoenix and Sienna.

Soon Millie and Darren join us.

I realize that a dorm management mix-up, an overprotective older brother, two complete opposites, and a first love that was almost ruined have found their happy ending after all.

About the author

Of course, it was sports - specifically ball games - that led Mrs. Kristal to writing. She started writing stories in 2012, and her first attempts at writing about soccer evolved over the years into real stories and eventually books.

Mrs. Kristal then switched continents and began writing about American football. In 2021, she published her first book about college romance and football. Mrs. Kristal draws inspiration from everyday situations, memories of experiences, and conversations with friends and family.

In addition to sports, her books are always about love and friendship. What she loves most about writing is being able to immerse herself in other worlds, taking her characters on a long journey, with a happy ending at the end. When Mrs. Kristal is not writing, she spends time with her friends and family and travels the world. One of her greatest wishes is to see the countries, cities, and stadiums she writes about at least once in her life.

Our books are also available in e-book. Find our catalog on:
https://cherry-publishing.com/en/

Editorial manager: Audrey Puech
Composition & Layout: Cherry Publishing
Interior illustrations: © Shutterstock
Cover design: Keti Matakov
Cover illustration: Keti Matakov

Made in the USA
Columbia, SC
06 August 2024

40071884R00124